T4-ADM-666

WHY AND HOW SECULAR SOCIETY SHOULD ACCOMMODATE RELIGION

A Philosophical Proposal

WHY AND HOW SECULAR SOCIETY SHOULD ACCOMMODATE RELIGION
A Philosophical Proposal

Edmund F. Byrne

The Edwin Mellen Press
Lewiston•Queenston•Lampeter

Library of Congress Cataloging-in-Publication Data

Byrne, Edmund F., date
 Why and how secular society should accommodate religion : a philosophical proposal / Edmund F. Byrne.; [with a foreword by Herbert Richardson].
   p. cm. -- (hors serie)
 Includes bibliographical references and index.
 ISBN-13: 978-0-7734-3811-8
 ISBN-10: 0-7734-3811-4
 1. Religion and sociology 2. Religion and state. I. Title.
 BL60.B97 2010
 306.6--dc22
                                     2009050462

hors série.

A CIP catalog record for this book is available from the British Library.

Copyright © 2010 Edmund F. Byrne

All rights reserved. For information contact

        The Edwin Mellen Press   The Edwin Mellen Press
        Box 450   Box 67
        Lewiston, New York   Queenston, Ontario
        USA 14092-0450   CANADA L0S 1L0

The Edwin Mellen Press, Ltd.
Lampeter, Ceredigion, Wales
UNITED KINGDOM SA48 8LT

Printed in the United States of America

Table of Contents

Foreword by Herbert Richardson — i

Acknowledgements — v

Introduction — 1

Part I. Religion under Secular Statecraft — 7

    Chapter 1. Rationalist Restrictions on Public Discourse — 11

    Chapter 2. Reasonable Limits on Religious Freedom — 25

    Chapter 3. The Hidden Dangers of Civil Religion — 39

Part II. State/Religion Border Control — 49

    Chapter 4. Religion-State Relations in U.S. Courts — 51

        Rulings concerning Religion-State Relations
        Rulings on Religion-State Relations in Education

    Chapter 5. Alternative Schooling in America — 65

Part III. Religious Groups and the Public Sphere — 80

    Chapter 6. The Political Importance of Interest Groups — 82

    Chapter 7. The Moral Need for Groups in a Modern Democracy — 94

    Chapter 8. Religious Groups in the Political Process — 106

Summary and Conclusion — 118

References — 126

Index — 134

FOREWORD

In this book Edmund Byrne seeks to justify a place for religion in public affairs. This is a timely and controversial topic to address.

Religious materials generated for consumption by the faithful still find many readers. There is a stable market for the sacred texts of both major and minor religions. Moreover, scholars who study textual and other problems of concern to followers of these religions attract readers who appreciate their more reflective musings. Then, too, a still more focused market exists for works based on archeological, anthropological, or historical research aimed at uncovering the origins of religious beliefs and practices. Are there, however, any supra-denominational topics *about* religion that still merit serious scholarly consideration?

This is admittedly a somewhat loaded question given that debate about whether religions should still exist is a growth industry spawned by interlocutory agnostics and apologists. Among scholars who prefer speaking to other scholars, this debate takes the form of arguments for and against the proposition that there is a God – or, alternatively, that a God has any interest in the inhabitants of this Earth whose place in this immense cosmos is so infinitesimal. Works that focus on the political significance of religion, however, address an issue that concerns many people whether they are believers or not. For, political power is more dependent on religious connections today than at any time in the past.

Throughout history a person's career opportunities in the public arena were often dependent on religious affiliation. The Enlightenment sought to replace sectarian preferences with reason-based secularism in matters political. And this, some think, has been achieved in most Western European and North American polities. Many Southern Hemisphere countries, though, continue to work out their political arrangements with attention to religious preferences. Catholicism prevails in much of Latin America. In predominantly Muslim countries religious minorities are often disenfranchised and even persecuted by the sect exercising political control (e.g., in Iraq, Iran, Lebanon, and even Israel).

In the United States, separation of church and state is supposed to provide a framework for avoiding religion-focused controversy. This secularist solution has never been more than an ideal, however. It has been repeatedly contested on many levels. And in recent decades a politically active religious right has created a powerful minority whose goal is to return government on all levels to its alleged Christian origins.

Even those open to such a transformation must see a need for caution if they give thought to the many excesses perpetrated by extremists in the name of their version of Christianity – or, alternatively, of Islam. Thus have American philosophers, especially liberals, long argued that only an unwavering secularism can keep church and state duly separate. Edmund Byrne – a philosopher who considers himself a liberal – interjects his voice into this debate to argue for a more nuanced and open-ended relationship between religious groups and governmental processes.

In Part I of this study, Byrne reviews the secularist model favored by many American philosophers, then provides some detailed examples of religion-based excesses in the United States. These complications duly noted, he then qualifies their significance by reminding readers that unconstrained secularism often engenders the intolerant excesses of civil religion.

In Part II Byrne, who also trained as a lawyer, homes in on the jurisprudential history of how US courts have gone about setting appropriate legal limits to religious influence in America's publicly funded schools.

Calling this juridical challenge a matter of "border control," he shows that courts in the United States have gradually become more accommodating of religious groups in K-12 settings. In times past, though, court rulings required public schools to be quite rigorously secular, so religious groups like the Roman Catholics founded schools whose curriculum included religious instruction.

In Part III Byrne returns to more philosophical considerations to carve out a place for religion in political affairs. Drawing on the sociopolitical debate about group rights, he argues that a commitment to church/state separation need not preclude religious groups from participating in governmental processes. To contextualize this argument, he first indicates that it is hardly possible to influence government in the modern world without operating in and through groups ("interest groups"). Then he addresses a variety of moral difficulties that a political system faces if it is open to group-generated input. This discussion grounds group politicization in the real world and thereby makes clear that Byrne's supportive stance is not naively open-ended. He is nonetheless persuaded that worthy causes (as well as others) can be better advanced by organized groups than by unconnected individuals. Finally, he cites various examples of religious groups that bring their preferences to bear on government in ways that are arguably appropriate whether espoused by religious or non-religious groups.

Should such activism be endorsed? Yes, within bounds, Byrne concludes. These bounds should be based, though, not "on the fact that the questing group has religious ties" but "as with any other interest group on arguments in opposition to the position being touted."

This carefully argued affirmation of a political place for religious groups steers adroitly between both sectarian and secularist bias to spell out reasons why a group that is organized around a religious motif should neither be summarily excluded from nor exceptionally favored in deliberations as to governmental policy and practice. It tacitly adopts as leitmotiv the ideal of democracy, which no government (surely none in the United States) has fully achieved. Even a call for an approximation of this ideal is nonetheless a welcome contrast to the more strident voices that urge their religion-oriented hearers to employ any means available to them to fulfill their ultimate political aspirations. Hopefully, these program-oriented activists – as well as politically sensitive philosophers – might find in this work some thoughts worth making their own.

Herbert Richardson, Ph.D.
The Edwin Mellen Press

ACKNOWLEDGEMENTS

This work is something of a hybrid in its origins. Like any work that draws on the scholarship of others, I owe a debt to many other authors. Most of them are cited under References. This work is not, however, just a product of reading and taking notes but has grown out of my living and experiencing different ways of organizing one's life. As is intimated en passant in the text, I was raised in an organized religion, studied for and assumed a ministerial role in that religion; then, after obtaining advanced degrees, I pursued an academic career in secular universities. Both phases of my life brought me in contact with influential individuals and their organized groups, some of which were religious and others secular. How these contacts took place and evolved over time contributed significantly to my understanding of the topics addressed in this book and the conclusions I reach. I do draw on a lot of scholarly research about groups; but I have also benefitted from interacting with other individuals in various groups. For, their approaches to identifying and solving problems have taught me to differentiate positive and not so positive aspects of how a group can influence and impinge upon one's life.

My appreciation of the positive influence of religion on a person's life is due in large part to my experiences among family members including my long widowed mother, teachers on all levels of the educational hierarchy, and random individuals who came to play a role in my maturation by exposing me to diverse worldviews not all of which were religious. Some must remain anonymous -- either because I no longer remember their names or because of privacy considerations, e.g., a devoted Catholic family man who was in charge of certain CIA operations in Europe and a former nun who became one of the world's leading experts on risk assessment.

Those who need not remain anonymous include several exceptionally dedicated philosophy professors who taught me by example how to be an intellectual (Edward Maziarz, a priest, and Jean Ladrière, a layman), and several professors who helped me recognize that religion does have content susceptible to scholarly discourse and dissemination (especially Mahlon H. Smith III and Tony Sherrill). A number of other individuals by their very way of living introduced me to the complex possibilities of human existence apart from any one religious outlook: a retired French cellist who was a Marxist; a noblesse oblige Belgian wine merchant (Michel Boon); a Jewish woman who had survived the Holocaust and was studying to become a doctor (Anne Potts); a warmhearted agnostic logician (John Riteris) who escaped Russian-occupied Latvia and lived long enough for me to know him thanks to a kidney donated by his twin brother; an Israeli political philosopher who has spent time in jail rather than participate in his country's military occupation of Palestine (Ovadia Ezra); and an academically successful woman who has shared many years of my life, improved my writing immeasurably, and quietly drawn me into her Episcopalian world (Anne Donchin).

In addition to the influence of individuals I have also come to better understand the issues addressed in this book precisely because of my experiences as a member of various groups. Chief among these groups are: the Roman Catholic Church in its US Midwest and its Belgian manifestations; and academe as represented primarily by institutions in the US Midwest (Illinois, Michigan, Wisconsin, and Indiana) and in Belgium, among which is included a law school. Also revelatory were my experiences in a religious novitiate and in several different seminaries and parishes, my involvement with labor unions and labor studies courses, and with various professional organizations that cultivate specialized philosophical studies. Also significant was my association with an international house for university students in Belgium (Maison Saint-Jean), with the Senior Law Project of the Indianapolis Legal Services Organization, with an education-oriented tourist organization that caters to seniors (Exploritas), and with *The Journal of Business Ethics*.

Also influential, as noted, were many scholars who crossed my path, in the flesh or in their writings, among whom I must include the focus and target of my doctoral dissertation, Thomas Aquinas. And now some forty years later my gratitude extends to the Edwin Mellen Press and its perceptive editor, Professor Herbert Richardson, who is himself a specialist in early medieval philosophy.

Introduction

As far back in time as we can trace the activities of homo sapiens this species of ours has been very busy sacralizing various things and various actions in an effort to direct otherwise uncontrollable events to favorable outcomes. This process, as studied by archeologists, anthropologists, and others, consisted of rites, invocations, and practices as varied as facial scarring and cannibalism, human sacrifice and homicidal games. Eventually symbols came to be used more prominently as practices evolved into what we think of as modern religions. What matters here is the seemingly universal fact that a group's religious practices were overseen by select individuals who had been taught how to conduct these practices and could in turn teach this to others. In this way a group maintained the continuity so essential to its well-being.

The official processors of a group's rites and ceremonies went by various names that still endure in today's vocabulary of religion: priests, imams, rabbis, shamans, witch doctors, whatever. Typically they were not identical with the political leaders as such, but their functions were coordinated with those of the political leaders. This functional duality persisted even as the respective tasks became more complex and eventually separated into the institutions that have for many centuries been thought of as state and religion. How each is expected to relate to the other is anything but obvious, however, and accordingly the task of establishing parameters has occupied people's attention for centuries.

For present purposes, the approaches taken to this task can be reduced to two: either by words or by actions. People with scholarly leanings have looked to words for this purpose; others, especially those with political objectives, have tended to rely on action. This has been preeminently true of states that prioritize uniform, manageable behavior within the territory they control. In Western Europe, at least, scholarship has never been the determining factor in a state's decision as to which worldview to favor. Rather has scholarship's political function been limited to articulating rationales for positions a state has taken for other reasons.

More broadly stated, worldviews do not determine how power is to be exercised; power determines what worldview will be officially encouraged within its jurisdiction. In countries where a religion other than Christianity, e.g., Islam, has been preeminent, selection of the state's official ideology is sometimes fought over with all the vehemence once common in the West. Meanwhile in the West most governments have sought to minimize such turmoil by adopting some version of secularism as their official ideology (Rémond 1999). In fact, a secularist worldview has been adopted as the official governmental posture in just about all North American and European countries.

This secularist stance, however, has functioned differently under different historical circumstances. In a country where secularism has replaced Christianity as the official ideology, e.g., France, any upsurge of an exotic religion once deemed hostile, such as Islam, is seen as a threat to established values. In a country whose government simply acknowledges no ties to religion, e.g., Turkey, Cuba, or the former Soviet Union, any evidence of marginal religious power generates controversy. For example, in Turkey recently a Muslim was subjected to bad press exposure when he ran for and was elected president. Even though a majority of the people in Turkey are Muslim, the officially secular government must appear to be rigorously neutral even as it judiciously accommodates the dominant religion. This sort of respectful accommodation is not to be confused, however, with the traditional religious state that maintains political power in part by equating citizenship rights with the preferred orthodoxy. Against such a state-religion marriage secularists everywhere brace themselves, even as they concede religious citizens various prerogatives they deem politically harmless.

There are at present a number of states each of which is partial to a major religion (Islam: Saudi Arabia = Judaism: Israel = Hinduism: India); but legal constraints in such countries tend to focus more on practice than on beliefs. Both

Israel and Ireland, for example, are gradually becoming less monolithic in their support of religious morality. The same is true of some states with large Muslim populations, e.g., Indonesia. Inversely, no religion-legitimated state is likely to be any more hostile to free expression than are states that enforce secular orthodoxy, as did both superpowers during the Cold War era. In earlier times, states defined blasphemy and heresy as noncompliance with religious orthodoxy and punished ideological noncompliance as a threat to their political power.

The political power in question here is sometimes internal and sometimes external to the organized religion, and so it has been over time. For thousands of years state and religion operated together to mutually reinforce one another for the sake of maintaining and as need be sharing power. Over time this relationship of mutual reinforcement became analogous to that of a master (the state) and a slave (the religion). After all, the former usually controlled the means of coercion – as illustrated in recent times by the spectacle of well-armed soldiers versus saffron-robed monks in Burma. The Burma/Myanmar situation is, however, something of an anomaly. For in many countries, including all members of the European Union, the once common practice of wedding a religion to a political power has been largely abandoned. In its place is an arrangement wherein the state's decision-making processes are assiduously cut off from the influence of religious spokespersons. This secularist arrangement seldom hermetically seals statecraft from religious intervention; nor does it always preclude the state from interfering with people's religious freedom. But the intent is clear if not even-handed. So its fulfillment is possible in the course of time. At least with respect to Christians and secularists it is for all practical purposes a fait accompli in Europe and by extension in some other countries as well. It is otherwise, however, in Arab nations; and secular states like Turkey and Indonesia are unofficially Islamic. Meanwhile, the state-religion relationship in the United States remains a work in progress.

The separation of state and religion is an established policy of the United States. To this end its founders appended to its Constitution an amendment that guarantees both "free exercise" and "nonestablishment" of religion. As interpreted over two centuries, this First Amendment is less rigorous in its ramifications than is Article X of France's Declaration of the Rights of Man, which decrees that "No man may be harassed because of his opinions, even religious ones" (Rémond 1999: 39). The latter in any event set in motion a turbulent historical process the result of which today is a secular state in most European countries. On this side of the Atlantic, meanwhile, the First Amendment first of all caused onetime colonies to end their official religion as they entered the union and required thereafter that no new state have an official religion. Federal courts have overseen the maintenance of this separation of religion from the state over the years, especially with regard to education. But many people, especially in the South, do not look kindly on this dichotomy. As various Evangelical and Pentecostal denominations become ever more numerous and widespread their followers envision a time when America will again be what they believe it was at its origins: a Christian nation. And those among them who are inspired by dominion theology look upon this outcome as no less than God's plan for the United States.

This sectarian vision of religion's destiny in the United States conflicts with the pluralist vision that is still preeminent; but it is by no means inconsequential. It has become a significant factor in electoral politics and in the formulation of public policy. Moreover, some of its leaders fully expect to move beyond selective influence to outright control of the government. Given the chaotic turmoil that European and, indirectly, pre-Revolutionary American polities went through before reaching the workable separation of state and religion that now prevails, no simple about-face is historically defensible. But neither is political suppression of religionists' altogether appropriate interest in public policy formation. So how is their interest to be accommodated without reopening our political institutions to undue sectarian influence?

To answer this question I will regard state/religion relations as an ethical issue that has not really been settled by the institutional divorce between state and religion.

In Part I, I will examine and critique the arguments American philosophers put forward in support, for the most part, of a worldview-neutral secular government. In Part II, I will similarly cast a critical eye on the US judiciary's attempts to fine-tune the neutrality worldview it deems called for by our Constitution. In particular, I part company with individualist interpretations of these efforts and propose in their stead an approach that takes group rights into account. This revisionist model is at the helm in Part III. There I contend that recognition of group rights provides an opening to some alternative social arrangements in which variously organized groups, religious and otherwise, are able to influence affairs of state responsibly and productively.

PART I
RELIGION UNDER SECULAR STATECRAFT

In a society in which no one worldview is shared by everyone, there should be limits on what adherents of a particular worldview may do to convert others to their beliefs and/or to achieve one-sided dominance over democratic government. Thus have various rules been proposed that aim to favor pluralism among worldviews and neutrality of preference on the part of government. In practice, however, neutrality is a will-o'-the-wisp. It does not apply to capitalism, for example, since this worldview is widely equated with correct thinking. Nor does it apply to such shibboleths as national defense, which is associated with a worldview labeled patriotism. No, the worldviews to which rules of neutrality are directed are for the most part those espoused by faith-based organizations. To be sure, religious worldviews are not all treated equally in comparison to preferred political worldviews or to one another. In part because religious groups have not all appeared on the scene at the same time, they do not all have comparable political access and voice nor do all enjoy freedom of speech and assembly to the same degree. Thus the politics of pluralism inevitably deviates from its theoretical model. Do the deviations invalidate the model, as some claim? At first glance, it seems they do. So where does tolerance come in?

Pluralism requires tolerance; and tolerance is a creature of trial and error. When first made a benefit provided by the nation-state, tolerance was greeted by former inter-religion combatants as the worst possible arrangement except for what they had just endured. In time, government leaders saw it as a sine qua non for redirecting people's energies to more productive endeavors. Now it is largely taken for granted, at least among liberals. But the fortress their forebears erected for its protection is under siege. In particular, its opponents claim that pluralism concedes too much to individual liberty and by so doing drains the meaning from people's lives. There is no arbiter-at-large, however, to say whether this is really the case and, if so, what should be done about it.

Few nation-states oversee only people who live by the same basic beliefs. Efforts to impose such uniformity by force often prove disastrous, and many of these can now be branded experiments that failed. With the demise of supra-ethnic combinations, new nations may yet reemerge in forms we can scarcely imagine. Western democracies, meanwhile, typically encompass differing groups that are required to accommodate one another for their common good. Though not impossible to sustain (historically, Switzerland has been a fine example), accommodation may give way to relationships of dominance and dependency. And in that sort of context evaluations of one group by another typically lack balance and forbearance. But is there any way to avoid this all too human bias? Consider the obstacles.

Groups are formed and maintained for different reasons. Sometimes people organize into groups to achieve a symbiosis of mutual interest and benefit, without regard to outsiders. Sometimes they organize to help others, sometimes to harm them. Sometimes they confuse one goal with the other. Sometimes there is much discussion as to which kind of goal a group is in fact pursuing, and judgments are made about the group's likely effect on anything from the governmental to the environmental aspects of people's live. Sometimes this evaluative process involves legal intervention, e.g., to identify a group as law abiding or in violation of law with respect to, say, payment of taxes or disposal of waste. In short, we routinely devote more time and attention to assessing groups than we realize. The threat we think they pose varies with circumstances, of course; but when we fear that our own well-being is at stake we are seldom open-minded.

When suddenly called upon to evaluate a group that we believe poses an immediate threat to our perceived interests, we may label its members as weird, perverse, crime-prone, or, as in the case of immigrants, simply illegal. This process of evaluation is analogous to what law enforcement personnel are expected to engage in, albeit (one hopes) more professionally. But the circumspection they should exercise may be superseded when large or at least influential segments of a society actively categorize and rate groups. Labels may be too freely assigned if the emotion of the moment is allowed to overwhelm reason But, after all, human beings have been doing just that from their origins. The resulting behavior takes many forms, one being, as noted, a privatization of sectarian preferences. This privatization is debatable on many scores, however, including just how truly neutral are the forces behind it. Surely religious freedom must be contained if it is so exercised as to threaten people's very survival. But such containment is hardly defensible when in the name of fairness and impartiality the worldview of law-abiding citizens is marginalized. So there are good reasons for reflecting on the pros and cons of secular neutrality. In particular, the secular model of a pluralist society needs fine-tuning.

Chapter 1

Rationalist Restrictions on Public Discourse

People who think religion should be excluded from public discourse are for the most part secularists. They base their opinion on what reason alone, without the aid of any sectarian beliefs, is able to discern. Thus they consider themselves rationalists; and this rationalist position of theirs makes them most comfortable with a secular model of governance. This secular model allows for the possibility that some unprovable beliefs will be shared by all citizens of a given state. These, according to the secular model, they may voice in the public arena. However, people who have group-specific beliefs that are not shared by all are expected to restrict their public discourse to assertions that are consistent with norms accepted by all. On the basis of laws enacting this secular model of governance, religion is officially privatized in most Western democracies.

At first glance this privatization of religion may seem unduly harsh. But it is an understandable reaction against what can happen when a religion is subsumed by the state. Take, for example, how the Roman Empire misused Christianity for political gain. For centuries the Roman emperors relied for political stability on a version of polytheism largely borrowed from the Greeks. Then the Emperor Constantine decided that Christianity could serve this purpose even more effectively. This it did for a time, as Charlemagne and others brought the new faith to infidels all over Europe at the point of a sword. "Christian" soldiers spread death and destruction to the Middle East as well. But their holy bloodbaths, later called crusades, failed to prove the falsity of Islam and barely kept this religion from spreading throughout the Iberian Peninsula.

Christianity itself was eventually subjected to rival interpretations that conveniently met the needs of newly forming nation-states that exploited for their own ends one or another competing interpretation of the original Gospel. As schisms and invasions incrementally undermined Rome's preeminence, the papacy turned to secular means, including military intervention, to bring rebellious city states into line. This secular misappropriation of spiritual purposes continued in one form or another even into the twentieth century, when Vatican City was established. The imperial pretensions of Roman Catholicism had already been nationalized, however, during the Reformation. At that time, secular princes localized the earlier Church's melding of doctrine and duty, each determining within his or her own domain which belief system was politically correct and which exposed one to death or imprisonment on a charge of heresy or blasphemy (Levy 1993). The content of such crimes was subject to change, however, if a different religion assumed the throne. This not infrequent occurrence was generally brought about in the usual non-theological way: through armed contest for God and country.

The Christian sectarianism that emerged during the Protestant Reformation, then, provided emerging secular powers in Europe with discrete ideologies on the basis of which their armies could spill one another's blood to determine whose souls were dearer in the sight of God. As new military tactics and weaponry achieved their deadly purposes, rulers whose populations had been decimated began to suspect that God had put a curse on all their houses. So they entered into a truce that ended religion-based hostilities. This did not prevent them from exploring for new reasons to engage in organized carnage; but it did lower the political intensity that had been associated with religious differences. One aspect of their solution was state-determined creedal priorities, which eventually gave way in most polities to a separation of religion and state (Rémond 1999). As embodied in the concept of liberalism, this requires government to tolerate any religion that claims adherents in the polity and is itself tolerant of others (e.g., Rousseau 1954, 4:8).

Liberalism thus understood requires government to be officially neutral as to religious preference. In actual practice, though, this neutrality is often indistinguishable from secularism. Secularism has in turn become a guiding principle in all Western-style democracies that are established among people whose diversity discourages state-enforced uniformity of belief and practice. But if secularism itself is a worldview, its potential for oppressing liberty is no less than that of any religious orthodoxy.

That said, secularist uniformity has never been implemented altogether successfully. Not even in states under Communist rule that officially favored atheism and actively suppressed religious groups, that is, first in the Soviet Union and then in mainland China. More flexible accommodations of doctrinal differences have evolved in Western countries. These include tolerating open expression of religious beliefs and practices, subject to such constraints as community and especially court oversight may impose. Such essentially privatized accommodations, however, fail to satisfy religious nationalists. Many Christian conservatives, for example, look upon political secularism as a mechanism whereby hostile forces frustrate God's plan to bring them to political power. Islamists in other countries feel, with even more reason historically, that political secularism is directly aimed at suppressing them (see, e.g., MacFarquhar 2003). In other words, many religion-involved people in different cultural settings are persuaded that secularist politics has woven the cloth of the polity too tight for sectarian comfort. But there are good arguments for saying this is as it should be. Addressing this issue is an ongoing challenge for intellectuals.

As envisioned by liberal academics, the secularist project of keeping religion privatized involves limiting the kinds of reasons that a government dedicated to secular standards may consider. Some adherents of this doctrine are too blatantly anti-religious to be associated with official neutrality. They may not go so far as to approve of the infamous Twelve who made reason their justification for mass murder as they directed the Reign of Terror in France. But one author warns that religion uncontained "is inherently intolerant and persecutory" (Marshall 1993: 854). Others use a less biased model of political secularism. Aiming to maintain the prerogatives of reason in a pluralist society, they proffer criteria for screening arguments that may be articulated in public debate.

Some proposed criteria are substantive, others are just procedural. A well-known proponent of the former is political philosopher John Rawls, who sought to identify substantive moral norms of public reason respect for which would facilitate maintaining a well-ordered society of free and equal citizens. Over time he gave his screen a wider mesh, but it would still block many kinds of argument from getting a hearing (Reidy 2000). He was open, however, about the philosophical sources from which he derived his theoretical preferences. Other liberal theorists say they merely wish to create a set of procedures that are available to all and favor none. In this way, they believe, they can prevent a government from favoring the constituents of any nongovernmental organization to the detriment of others less favored.

These theorists, in other words, make "procedural neutrality" their operational ideal. To achieve it they recommend limiting public discourse to what all can be asked to hear without giving undue preference to any sectarian belief not shared by all. Proposals differ as to how forgiving the (anonymous) gatekeeper can be in this regard, but most approach this political question as though it were really epistemological. One, for example, would tolerate a religious view in the public arena if it has a secular reason and is put forward with secular motivation and rationale. Another cites the inability of any doctrine to monopolize the truth as justification for seeking through open debate possible areas of congruity or compromise. A third would admit into political discourse only those aspects of group-specific beliefs that are common to any and all other belief systems represented among the populace of a nation-state. (Carter 1993.)

Philosopher Robert Audi, for one, has convinced that "religious and other liberties" are best preserved if the proponent of a position in the public forum is motivated by and appeals only to adequate secular (nonreligious) reasons and the authority deciding what is to be done relies for this purpose only on secular considerations. This schema for secular policy-making yields what Audi thinks of as three principles: secular motivation; secular rationale; and secular resolution (1989a; 2000). That, it would seem, comes down to saying that the entire process should be unqualifiedly secular. But by whose standards? Who, for example, is to decide whether a stated reason is <u>adequately</u> secular? An ecclesiastical and a government representative might well differ about this; so Audi now tries to make allowances for such differences (2000).

Other liberal theorists would like to make perfect neutrality the standard of political discourse, notably by insisting that only "accessible" arguments be spoken and heard. Not to be confused with physical accessibility, of concern to the disabled, what is at issue here is intellectual accessibility. By definition, an argument is intellectually accessible if it can be understood without benefit of any special faith or revelation. Towards this end, says philosopher Thomas Nagel (1987), a public official should treat everyone alike not oppressively but on the basis of beliefs that can be shown to be "justifiable from a more impersonal standpoint" that operates out of "a higher standard of objectivity."

Nagel's intent in this regard is understandable, namely, to prevent public officials from coercing people unfairly on the basis of reasons that are not meaningful to all. His proposed remedy would hardly be easy to set up, though. How, in particular, would faith-based arguments be screened for access to public debate? Apparently Nagel would have everyone do what any responsible philosopher would do, that is, "submit one's reasons to the criticism of others" in order to reach, he presumes, a higher-order impartiality. But who would decide if the objectivity and impartiality attained is sufficient – and on the basis of what beliefs (Thurley nd)? And why shouldn't some such screening process be applied to any principled nonconformity, such as some citizens' refusal to pay taxes aimed at what they consider an immoral use?

It should not, of course, because such broad screening would surely engender an unduly doctrinaire uniformity, e.g., with regard to any work of art not acceptable to all citizens. This, moreover, would be altogether contrary to what liberal neutralists hope to achieve. One in particular, Charles Larmore, longs for a "neutral justification of political neutrality," by which he means one that does not itself rest on any controversial conception of the good (1987: 53). For, he argues, people tend naturally to disagree among themselves about what constitutes the good life; and, this being the case, a liberal society needs to find a way to accommodate "reasonable disagreement" short of resorting to force (1996, chs. 6-7; see Young 2002)

The neutrality approach to pluralism, then, calls for criteria of admissibility that will keep beliefs not susceptible to rational support out of public deliberations. Considered in the abstract, where many philosophers "hang out," this project perhaps merits consideration. After all, its proponents are manifestly conscientious about it, seeking as they presumably do only what is best for all citizens however diverse their mental states may be. But, truth be told, what they propose is not now and perhaps never will be practicable outside the ivory tower. For, in the real world where political strategies are devised and people engage in the activities whereby political power is obtained and used, religious commitments have influenced governmental outcomes for centuries. Thus it has taken several centuries to establish secular systems among all members of the European Union (Rémond 1999). In the United States the Constitution sets limits on state/religion interchange. But this has in no way kept presidents from invoking divine guidance (Domke and Coe 2008). Nor has the conservative right been deterred from organizing its adherents politically and directing them towards political dominance (Philips 2006, Pt. II).

Compared to the political upsurge of religious worldviews in various parts of the world, the threat of secular hegemony is arguably less problematic now than it was before the fall of the Soviet Union or the rise of a capitalist China. But the world has not become so benign that the potential danger of politicized secularism can be ignored (see below). Concentrating as they do on sectarian beliefs not shared by all citizens, liberal scholars do not concern themselves with partisan political differences, nor do they examine the worldview within which their meticulous logicality supposedly resides. Having abstracted from this worldview in order to engage in normative reflection "from nowhere," in Nagel's remarkable expression, they focus philosophical attention on second-order questions about political discourse rather than on any first-order question raised within religion or, for that matter, politics (see Kleinberg 1991:10-12). Yet they would provide political activists with rules of rhetorical propriety that are derived unblushingly from secular liberalism.

In light of this veiled hypocrisy, Alasdaire MacIntyre was generally on target when he called liberalism "a political doctrine about what cannot be justified and what ought not to be permitted: interference of a variety of kinds with individual liberty" (1971: 282-83). MacIntyre attributed this exclusionary attitude on the part of liberals to their inveterate antipathy to state-sponsored religions that prevailed during the *ancien regime* until terminated after the French Revolution of 1789. But a no less plausible explanation is their unstated assumption that only religious beliefs lead to persecution, strife, and bloodshed. To indulge this assumption, surely, one would have to ignore secularist suppression of alternative political views (e.g., in China, Turkey, Syria, Egypt, and Myanmar/Burma); for this also foils liberal aspirations.

A liberal polity that practices ideological neutrality might be somewhat open to expressions of sub-societal beliefs in the public sphere if the beliefs in question are shared by all participants in the public discourse (Galston 1991 pt. 2). Similarly, liberals' belief that their vision of neutrality deserves to be implemented is itself a special commitment, so any public utterance in its support would also fail an unbiased application of the neutrality test. This, however, is less a principled mandate than a recipe for rhetorical etiquette. Following a different recipe, a member of the Indiana General Assembly who knew his constituents well once (1977) defended reinstating capital punishment by noting that its application to Jesus brought about the redemption of the entire human race.

As this linkage between capital punishment and redemption illustrates, even if one endorses liberal neutrality in principle, the task of locating the boundaries of public discourse remains formidable. Should they extend, for example, to a gathering on the mall in Washington, D.C., at which a Christian minister describes with biblical allusions his vision of a time when all Americans can thank God Almighty that they are free at last? Some would say yes, in the wake of 9/11/2001. But isn't the right of assembly involved and should it not be honored even in proximity to the locus of government? Or perhaps the restriction should be applied only to official government activities? If so, this should not be taken to mean that belief-inspired concerns would have no access, say, to judicial processes. After all, one might point out, since 2006 five of the nine US Supreme Court justices have been Roman Catholic. So maybe the legislative and executive branches should be neutralized? If so, how would one go about banning the expression of special views before any branch of government in the United States without curtailing people's First Amendment right to petition the government for redress of grievances?

For John Rawls, apparently, imposing such a ban on free speech was not a problem. He favored extending the ban to all governmental and quasi-governmental venues including political campaigns and even the act of voting (1993: 215-16). Since people are wont to vote their consciences, as the saying goes, such de facto censorship seems more akin to thought control than to political liberation. So is liberal neutrality a political ruse by means of which the only beliefs not heretical by definition are those acceptable to secularists? If so, it could not have accommodated some of the most important political transformations of recent decades, including some that arose out of deeply held religious convictions and led to comparatively liberal governments (Casanova 1994). For reasons such as these, secularist approaches to pluralism are regretted by many religionists, who call for correctives that range from moderate to radical.

Radical reformers consider secularism to be a false religion and would replace it with a form of government that embodies the one true religion to which, of course, they subscribe (Juergensmeyer 1993). Their goal, then, is to reintroduce the very establishment of religion that led first to religion-based wars and then to the secularist solution. The particular religion so favored would vary from one cultural setting to another. Islam is on offer in many developing countries; and analogous expectations are entertained by some Christian fundamentalist groups in the developed world, including the United States (Greenawalt 1995 ch. 9; Philips 2006, ch. 6).

Moderate reformers agree that state secularism may itself become or at least favor a form of religious orthodoxy, but they believe its bias can be overcome by requiring government to be more open to religious diversity even in the formation of public policy. The goal of moderate reform is accordingly somewhat diffuse as different proponents look for ways in which a state can accommodate diverse beliefs and practices without itself becoming an embodiment of any one of them. Scholars whose focus is on religious teachings as such tend to favor few if any constraints on use of and reference to religious beliefs in efforts to influence public policy (e.g., Hofrenning 1995). Inversely, scholars more supportive of the liberal exclusion from government forums of any sectarian or other group-specific beliefs favor more nuanced accommodations.

Law professor Kent Greenawalt, a longtime student of religion-state relations in constitutional law and himself a believing Christian, considers the norms and practices now being applied in the United States to be about all that is needed (1995: 6-7). Thus he favors ecumenical cooperation among mainstream religious groups, none of which is established, and equal toleration of and political limitations on more atypical groups whether religiously or non-religiously inspired. He disapproves of public officials' citing religious tenets to support their candidacy or policy recommendations. He approves of letting religious organizations bring their moral suasion to bear on important matters of public policy. He insists, though, that strongly held beliefs are no substitute for expertise in regard to fact-based policy considerations.

Greenawalt looks to an overlapping consensus or common ground among diverse groups as the area of intersection between "private consciences and public reasons." This area of intersection is identified by others as civil society, that is, the totality of non-coercive organizations and activities through which private citizens effect public good. On this view, the public good functions as a criterion for admission of an agent or activity into public discourse and is typically invoked to justify philanthropic activity in a secular society. John Rawls, by contrast, was wary of this crack in the door. His version of secular government (what he called "political liberalism") favored the perpetuation of nonpublic groups; but he opposed their direct involvement in public policy formulation as a threat to the stability of the body politic (Rawls 1993: xix, 10, 76, 106, 137, 220; Pakaluk 1994).

Allocating the proper reach of ideas between public and nonpublic discourse was crucial for Rawls. He would allow associations to address any issue within the confines of public reason. Indeed, after having rethought the public discourse of such leaders as Abraham Lincoln and Martin Luther King, Jr., he endorsed allowing even nonpublic ideas into public discussion. Moreover, he held that government should protect (reasonable) associations. Under protection, though, he did not include government funding or subsidizing of faith-based nonprofits – except perhaps to facilitate distributing welfare to the least advantaged. His priority in these matters was to safeguard the liberty interests of people in groups against oppressive intrusions. For, he felt, democracy would be doomed in a system in which any association not abolished outright is a part of government -- or what he called "the basic structure." That arrangement, he observed, is a defining characteristic of fascism, at least as established in Nazi Germany. To avoid this danger, Rawls relies on a government that "you and I" have set up to exercise "collective coercion" for the mutual advantage of "our" respective interests (1993: 189, 221n.8, 247-54, 261, 284-85, 328-29, 359-63).

Rawls, then, envisioned a society in which justice as fairness has become second nature for politically virtuous citizens, collective provision of basic rights-sustaining welfare has been institutionalized, and individuals and associations are free to thrive. He assures us, moreover, that this society is attainable, provided "we" depoliticize advocates of destabilizing ideas and would-be dominant interest groups and suppress those whose subversive advocacy is "realizable." This cautionary proviso pre-dated the introduction of intrusive antiterrorism surveillance in developed countries. And perhaps no reasonable group would have cause to fear such monitoring so long as it retains respect for what Rawls called tolerable liberty. Inversely, the tenets of liberalism, which originated as an antidote to religious wars, do not welcome into political discourse any nonpublic organization however philanthropic its motives (1993: xxv, 39, 62-64, 144-48, 187, 301-03, 311-12, 344).

Presumably alarmed by religion-touting bloodbaths around the world, Rawls wants to keep conflicts among "comprehensive doctrines" below the threshold of collective pain. This objective is commendable in principle; but in posing it he fails to solve the crucial problem of implementation. This is due in part to his conviction (formed prior to the counter-example of US-occupied Iraq) that neutrality is not only politically possible but is the only reliable path to successful democracy. Thus for him the political problem of diversity involves finding a way to maximize every citizen's (cooperative) freedom of speech and association while at the same time fortifying government decision making against unilateral indoctrination. This, he seemed persuaded, would not suppress but would actually facilitate reasonable nonpublic diversity. But the resulting "one unified system of social cooperation" that he envisioned would rely on government to coordinate the total contribution that diverse associations make to "public culture" (1993: 11, 40-43, 321-24). Thus, he believed, a government can function in a sufficiently disinterested manner to assure religious and ethnic minorities that they are as important to the body politic as their numbers justify.

This liberal ideal, long espoused in the West, has not fared well in countries made up of heterogeneous and hierarchically diverse populations, which is the case in much of the Southern Hemisphere and increasingly in the Northern as well. In particular, policies established in the United States decades ago to accommodate minorities fairly are no longer adequate as this country becomes markedly less homogeneous both ethnically and with regard to wealth distribution. Yet even those policies are now being opposed by denying there is a problem that required their introduction in the first place. In short, how government might coordinate diversity without succumbing to either secular or sectarian dominance is no easy question.

Rawls, to his credit, did seek a more accommodating answer (Bridges 1994). He thought a democracy can survive ideological diversity only if government limits its own bank of ideas to a consensual subset of aspirations. In this age of complex public/private partnerships, however, the public good is perhaps better achieved by diverse agents that are only indirectly tied to government. Some of these government certifies as nonprofit to maximize their resources both negatively (through tax exemption) and positively (through contributions and even subsidization). Rawls, however, would want any claim about such actions being for society's overall public good to be assessed only on the basis of public reason publicly operationalized.

Rawls thought a value-neutral government could referee the preferences of a pluralist society's disparate components. But the interests and priorities of government are inherently indifferent if not hostile to values and beliefs that favor alternative policies and practices. The latter, as formulated by a nongovernment organization, may not be more advantageous to society as a whole than are those defended by government. But the reverse is likely to be true if all nongovernment organizations are able to discuss and negotiate among themselves with regard to their most deeply held beliefs. This can be done in a flourishing civil society. As consensus is reached or at least approximated the weight of such considered opinion deserves the government's full attention. In other words, differences are better accommodated than neutralized, and an accommodating society is likely to be better in the long run for having done so.

Consider in this regard some different religion-based views that arguably call for different government responses. If the government has adopted bellicose policies it may not welcome opposition to its military activities; yet surely a plea to "give peace a chance" deserves the attention of the body politic, even if articulated, say, by church-goers. These same church-goers might also favor freedom-diminishing policies as they defend traditional lifeworlds and moral norms. They might also aspire to see their conception of the public good applied to all. But what they seek should not be rejected merely because based on their group-specific beliefs. They should in any event be taken seriously, especially when they address an issue of common concern, e.g., preventing corporate fraud or providing for children's health care. They in turn need to find ways to become what they potentially are: social gadflies committed to awakening in the community at large all the untapped possibilities of human dignity and fulfillment.

Neutrality, in conclusion, should not be a code word for a preferred orthodoxy that undermines the ability of other opinions to be heard in the public forum. Nor should the public forum be thought to include only government deliberation and decision making. It includes as well all opportunities made available in civil society, including pulpits, media presentations, and political activities of all kinds. More intense if not incestuous involvement of value-committed organizations with government will, many believe, be counterproductive in the long run. But in practice governments often hear them when they speak -- or, at least, when they act in ways that contribute to the public good. It should be otherwise only when they demonstrably do not.

Chapter 2
Reasonable Limits on Religious Freedom

I ended the first chapter saying that a government isn't obliged to listen to a group if it acts in ways that demonstrably don't contribute to the public good. This is an understatement, because some groups don't merely fail to contribute to but actively impair the public good. With regard to such a group a government may need to be not merely indifferent but intrusive. In other words, it may need to restrict the activities of a trouble-making group. Assuming that the trouble in question is serious, this statement is hardly controversial as a general rule. But what if the group in question claims to be religious? In that case religious freedom becomes an important consideration and toleration is in order – at least up to a point. Beyond that point a society needs to impose reasonable limits. So we need to ask ourselves what limits are reasonable.

Religion as personal belief and to some extent as an organized institution is now tolerated in many countries around the world. But this toleration does not apply to every religious practice. The US government, for example, recently tried to keep prisoners from reading religious books that might contain an anti-government thought (NYT 10 and 21 Sept. 2007). This misguided ban was soon lifted, and rightly so. Inversely, it is difficult at least in principle to fault government efforts to control a religion-based group that devotes itself to criminal behavior. And between these two extremes lies the problematic group that threatens only its own members.

It is comparatively easy to decide correctly how the extremes – very harmful and not harmful at all to society at large – should be handled. Leave the harmless group alone. As for the antisocial group, identify its threat to society at large and determine individuals' responsibility for that threat. The group that is harmful only internally is a separate issue. The importance of knowing when and how to limit harm a group does to its own members is exemplified by a government's reluctance to prosecute serious rights violations within an organization.

Antisocial groups are usually referred to, even by their members, as gangs. As applied to and by youth seeking status among peers, the term 'gang' should hardly be considered problematic. Gangs are problematic, however, if they engage in criminal activity. Over the past several decades such gangs have become the focus of law enforcement legislation in the United States. This in turn has led to a recognition that a criminal gang has religion-like features: not only organization or hierarchy and criminal goals but a common code of conduct and common beliefs and identifiers (Langston 2003). The extreme to which such a group can go is manifested in a Kenyan religion-based group called the Mungiki.

The Mungiki (meaning 'multitude') is an ethnically distinct, religion-based cult, once boasting half a million members. It broke off from the Tent of the Living God in the early 1990s, rejected Western values such as Christianity, and adopted traditional Kikuyu customs, including female genital cutting. It gradually gained control of taxis and garbage collection in Nairobi, took up protectionist practices that it enforces by beheading the noncompliant, and established a political arm called the Kenya National Youth Alliance. The government banned the Mungiki cult in 2002 and since then has been imprisoning some and (allegedly) killing other of its leaders. Even if not directly responsible for ethnic mayhem against the Masai following a contested election, this group hardly merits political immunity by virtue of its religious roots.

By contrast, governments are sometimes reluctant to intervene in behalf of individuals who are being severely mistreated within a group. For example, only after repeated complaints did Texas authorities intervene in 2008 in behalf of minor girls whom the leaders of a polygamous Mormon sect took as wives without their consent. A more notorious example involves the deaths of over 900 members of a group in Jonestown, Guyana, thirty years earlier. Disputed facts aside, this group began as the Peoples Temple in California, then in 1977 a thousand of its members went to Guyana to set up a religious socialist community.

Their leader, Reverend Jim Jones, portrayed this organizational arrangement as divine socialism the ultimate fulfillment of which would be revolutionary death (Chidester 2003, 56-60, 124-128). Most of his followers in Guyana seemingly accepted this worldview for themselves. It proved short-lived, however. In 1978 a U.S. Congressman went there to learn more about the group; and on that occasion he was killed and most members of the group also died – the latter apparently at their own hands. On this account, the group brought death upon itself. But conspiratorial theories about the role of the US government in their demise abound (Moore 2005).

Reverend Jones had religious roots in mainstream evangelical Protestantism. After moving from Indiana to San Francisco he maintained good relations with the city government and for a time he chaired the city's housing authority. But as he became involved in the problems of the poor, he transformed his religious beliefs into a Marxist worldview; and this led to his founding a Marxist-oriented community in Guyana. There he apparently exercised autocratic control over the men, women, and children (mostly black) who gave him all they owned. In return for their money, according to some accounts, Jones gave them a sense of self-importance, worth, and even grandeur. But some say that he gave these only to those who practiced self-denigration and unquestioning obedience.

Reliable records indicate that Jones trained the people in advance to carry out a mass suicide/infanticide. And in the end, according to this critical account, they did choose death rather than renounce the beliefs that gave their lives meaning. If so, their fate resembles that of the Jews who took their own lives at Masada rather than submit to the Romans, and Jews in tenth century York who did the same rather than yield to a mob of Christian bullies, and also Old Believers who did so in 17-18th century Russia rather than accept revisions of Russian Orthodoxy (Chidester 2003, 135-137). And so also did others, as Eric Schwarz-Bart reminds us in his novel *The Last of the Just*.

People also choose death indirectly by becoming participants in a "holy war" which by definition is set apart from ordinary conflicts because it is being fought for a sacred cause. This attitude is now associated most readily with Islamists; but it may be based on an unqualifiedly secular worldview, as was the case with imprisoned Italian Communist Antonio Gramsci, who endured his deteriorating health rather than request clemency and thereby acknowledge the authority of the government he opposed. And so also, we are told, did Jim Jones and his followers die rather than cave in to an oppressive government.

What clouds our understanding of the Jonestown incident are various conspiratorial claims regarding the extent of government intervention in the group's affairs. What exactly did U.S. Congressman Leo Ryan come down from California to investigate? Was it complaints about Jones mismanaging funds and keeping people against their will? Or was it rather reports about CIA misuse of the group? If in fact US CIA agents were present there, were they merely curious about the group's Marxist worldview or were they, as alleged, conducting mind control tests on group members (Wise n.d.)? Jones himself spoke openly about US government interference (Chidester 2003, 142-143); but post mortem investigations were inconclusive regarding these matters. So we are left with the standard story about an atypical religious group that, like others, chose suicide over surrender.

That an entire community of people would at one man's command knowingly swallow lethal doses of arsenic, as reported, is difficult to understand. But a questionably genuine tape recording of those final hours has Jones telling the people the U.S. Army would soon be parachuting in to finish them off. So if that is true he was offering them death with dignity plus an opportunity to embarrass the capitalists and advance the cause of Communism in the world. But it is unlikely that those people saw themselves as so down and out in the world that what Jones offered them seemed better by comparison. Besides, this self-deprecation thesis would explain only their initial attraction to Jones's group, not their apparent willingness to persevere in spite of the final immolation their leader was proposing. So we really need to probe more deeply for an adequate explanation.

Might we attribute their dedication and perseverance to mass hypnosis? Even if we knew exactly what happens when an individual is hypnotized, this would not explain how it is possible to hypnotize an entire group, as perhaps before a battle.

Nor would it enable us to prove that this has in fact occurred in a given instance. But how else can one account for the multiple deaths that occurred that day – 18 November 1978 – in Guyana? Did those people really know what they were doing? And if they did, why would they also kill their own children? Or were outsiders doing all this to them, possibly because of their Marxist leanings at the height of the Cold War? All we know for sure is that by the end Jones had become a paranoid autocrat and his slain followers had beliefs that were characterized as unpatriotic. These beliefs were of interest to the CIA, and Congressman Ryan had worked hard to contain CIA overreaching. So both psychological and political factors were involved in the tragic outcome. These factors alone do not fully explain what happened in Jonestown. But they do help explain other instances of arguably excessive US government intrusion on people's religious freedom.

One such instance occurred in 1992, when a neo-Nazi named Wheeler held out against US law enforcement agents at Ruby Ridge in Idaho and another a year later, when David Koresh's self-styled Branch Davidians were besieged outside Waco, Texas. In both instances the government's incursion had tragic results (82 of the latter were killed). What remains controversial are the criteria by which one decides whether the government's interference is appropriate. Some argue that the harm government causes when it interferes with people's right to exercise their religion freely militates against setting a limit on what practices are allowable when carried out for religious reasons.

This strong defense of religious freedom was illustrated in the American Civil Liberties Union's publication *Civil Liberties* shortly after the Jonestown tragedy. Its spokesperson's statement, I thought, was an uncritical whitewashing of every form of excess in the name of religion; so I sent them the following letter (here edited) for publication:

If [then ACLU director] Jeremiah Gutman's statement that "people have a right to believe any damn fool thing they like" represents the ACLU position on cults, as asserted in the February 1979 *Civil Liberties*, then ACLU is taking a simplistic approach to a very complex issue. For, it is only the <u>free</u> exercise of religion about which Congress shall make no law. Important as it may be to keep government from intruding into First Amendment rights, there is more to cults than just abstract beliefs coincidentally held in common by a group of individuals who freely choose to assemble together. These characterizations might be assumed prima facie; but they are rebuttable. For, also at issue is informed consent. The woman who withdraws all her money from the bank to give to a con artist in the belief that he is investigating an embezzler has a right to believe the con; but that doesn't give the con artist the right to practice fraud and deception to her detriment. Nor should concern about constitutional protections against undue government involvement hinder people's right to petition for redress of grievances. After all, some victims of the Final Solution may have believed they were being taken to work camps. Would you, then, have cut off all efforts to rescue them by tossing a mantle of "religion" over Eichmann's endeavors? Organized "religion" in short, is almost never just a set of ideas in somebody's head. So it should be subject to judicial review when it reaches the tip of somebody's nose.

My letter wasn't published; but the issue of immunity for anything labeled religious needed to be addressed, because by concentrating on government excesses the ACLU was disregarding harm caused in the name of religion. For, its self-selected mission was limited to defending constitutionally protected civil liberties. In so doing, it disregarded the social context of religious belief – in a way that the United States Supreme Court has seldom done (Donahue 1985, 1994).

As suggested, our courts sometimes subordinate the free exercise clause of the First Amendment to the public welfare as a whole. This prioritizing may affect well known and obscure groups alike, but the latter are more vulnerable to constraints. In 1982, for example, the U.S. Supreme Court held that Hare Krishna devotees who proselytized in public places, especially airports, were entitled to First Amendment protection, but were also subject to reasonable time, place, and manner restrictions: *Heffron v. International Society for Krishna Consciousness, Inc.*, 452 U.S. 640 (1982). (This ruling was based on a test announced in 1968 in *United States v. O'Brien*, 391 U.S. 367, 376: the free speech of any group, whether secular or sectarian, may be regulated provided that what is regulated is not the content of expression, is narrowly tailored to serve a significant government interest, and leaves ample alternative channels for communicating the information.)

Also in 1982 the Court ruled 5-4 against Minnesota's subjecting the Rev. Sun Myung Moon's Unification Church to special scrutiny just because more than one-half of its income came from non-members: *Larson v. Valente*, 456 U.S. 228. At about the same time, it held that the Pennsylvania Amish's religious beliefs did not exempt them from paying employees= social security taxes: *U.S. v. Lee* [455 U.S. 252], even though ten years earlier it had allowed the Amish in Wisconsin to withdraw their children from public schools after the eighth grade (*Wisconsin v. Yoder*, 1972). Then in 1989, in another 5-4 decision in *Hernandez v. Commissioner*, 490 U.S. 680, it upheld an Internal Revenue Service ruling that payments to the Church of Scientology for "auditing" sessions are not deductible contributions, even though, as Justice O'Connor noted in dissent, the I.R.S. does allow deductions to Mormons who pay for a "temple recommend" Jews who pay for a seat in temple on High Holy Days, and Catholics who pay mass stipends.

Even less likely to be accommodated are groups whose very existence is not clearly in the public interest. For instance, when the California drug addiction center known as Synanon turned to intra-group and extra-group violence to defend its interests, it lost its aura, its donors, and then its special claim to First Amendment protection against governmental monitoring. In a word, merely calling one's group religious affords no guarantee of immunity from governmental regulation. Nor should such immunity ever be facilely attained. The public good should be a controlling consideration. But the public good is a complex objective of human endeavor. So perhaps a few words about this are in order here.

Constructed in part out of past experience, the public good is also a projection of human aspirations. There is no one plan, though, for its advancement; and different plans may be utterly incompatible at least as implemented. Nor do all agree about the reasons for these differences. This basic feature of the human condition is better described by use of some images than others. In particular, it serves no purpose to envision any one-size-fits-all dosage of public good rolling off an assembly line in response to orders placed. Rather is the public good like a great bazaar, where different merchants entice buyers with their particular versions of betterment. Competition enters into all of this, but much less so than diversity.

So long as this diversity is distributed among different niches, the ecosystem of human well-being is sustainable. Dialogue open to diversity further enhances this tacit agreement to coexist. But the agreement falls on bad times if any occupant of a niche attempts to expand into other niches or redesign the ecosystem as a whole in its own image. Response from other niche occupants is inevitable, and often ungrateful; for, the disruption seldom leaves all unaffected. So advancement purportedly for all typically leaves some behind. It may even advance none of them, least of all the would-be revisionist.

Adding weight to these words, of course, is the human potential for violence, which some find appealing beyond words. But violence can quickly lose its luster when put to everyday use. None ever being fully fit, survival may then be a will-o'-the-wisp – unless perhaps violence can be countered by overwhelmingly greater violence. This at least is the modern (Hobbesian) basis for nation-states.

Nationalization of violence is the modern approach to controlling threats both within and beyond territory that is centrally administered. To use this approach effectively, however, the government of a nation-state must be able to distinguish friend from foe, both within and beyond the territory it governs. To assert that this approach has been successful internationally one must be able to show that a war may be a path to human well-being. Internal success, in turn, should be assessed within parameters set by totalitarian and anarchist extremes. The happy medium in this regard is arguably a liberal democracy; but even in such a polity a government's appraisal of groups is ever vulnerable to partiality and bias. Politics aside, such appraisal cries out for goal-sensitive criteria that can both guide and limit constraint.

In the United States, the First Amendment has been read as a limit on government's right to control groups. But the Constitution also obliges government to preserve ("insure") domestic tranquility. So to any endorsement of a group's autonomy is affixed an important caveat, namely, that the social order remain reasonably stable. Threats to that stability may require limiting the scope and methods of special advocacy. The grounds for outright suppression should be determined, however, not by government fiat -- as is now authorized under various post-9/11 statutes broadly interpreted -- but on the basis of input from all interested parties. The goal: to preserve the public good already achieved with no more diminution of anyone's liberty than the severity of threatened harm to others truly warrants.

This standard ode to freedom having been recited, it remains the case that groups committed to harming others may have great disruptive potential. This is the case whether their scope of operations involves the rise or fall of nations, the oppression or even annihilation of a disfavored minority, the organized mayhem of never finalized ethno-political realignments, or control of contested urban turf. Somewhat less dramatic are democratically pursued demands for increased ethnic autonomy, or the growing attraction of the more affluent to segregated, internally administered community associations, or the desire of politically active religious groups to set policy for schools and governments on all levels (Hofrenning 1995; Philips 2006: Pt. II). Inversely, both business and government entities sometimes secretly fund "grassroots" demonstrations and even ongoing organizations to advance their own undisclosed interests.

These and other challenges to popular democracy discourage reliance on groups to advance the public good; but they hardly justify a sweeping condemnation of groups as instruments of human betterment. Civilization however advanced is ever in need of reform. Truly participatory monitoring should enable us to distinguish between agendas that will and those that won't contribute to the public good. It should also help us discern among the latter those that won't internalize - strictures on civil disobedience. The problem here is that few groups perceive themselves to be anything but contributors to the public good -- even if what they do best is harm other people. Harm is one thing, however; identifying the aggressor (as is required by "just war" theory) is quite another.

To let government randomly support or suppress any group on arbitrary grounds opens the door to a totalitarian system in which none is safe, as is the case in many dictatorial states. Few defend such mass murderers as Hitler, Stalin, Idi Amin, or Pol Pot. But a government's abuse of its control over violence is likely to be tolerated, even in a democracy, so long as its status as a nation-state is popularly accepted as an absolute value to which all other values are subordinate. Thus have American citizens apparently gone along with its government's war-making activities since 9/11/2001. If the government exercising dominance over people's lives lacks this basic legitimacy, the foci of civility shift. Hostility can no longer be explained away as insubordination but must be seen as deriving at least in large measure from honorable claims to human rights.

Given the real but hyperbolically magnified threat from so-called terrorists, some future US government could impose military rule, however unlikely that might seem. Even in more ordinary times, we live as a people divided from one another in all kinds of ways, economic disparity being among the most polarizing factor. For the first century of the US's existence as a nation, nonpublic philanthropic activity provided the chief means of ameliorating this disparity. Then in the century that followed, the process of amelioration came to be heavily subsidized by government even as it continued to be carried out by nonprofits. Now this institutionalization of charity is coming undone; and as it does the conditions for popular resentment intensify. Civility thus will be under siege, and the grounds for tolerance will be sorely tested. On the basis of what reasonable criteria can the limits of tolerance be laid out?

Religious freedom is more respected in the United States than in many other countries. But the very concepts that have made this respect for religious freedom possible have also accommodated a right to be nonreligious, or secular. This, I contend, has until recently embodied the officially preferred set of values even to the point of constituting a kind of establishment in reverse. For the first several centuries of European incursions into North America the mainstream religion was Protestantism in its various, mostly northern European, configurations. Catholicism made inroads gradually, especially after the Irish and Italians began to migrate in large numbers in the latter part of the nineteenth century. Jews, though represented in the population from earliest times, have found it more difficult than others to secure their rights, though they have never been persecuted in this country as in

Europe. The same is true of numerically smaller groups, including Hindus and even Muslims. Indeed, our federal courts on occasion even take seriously non-churchgoing people variously identified as agnostics or non-believers or secular humanists.

Against this background of religious groups and responsible non-religious groups there is a tradition of U.S. Supreme Court decisions and their progeny in the lower courts that set limits to the free exercise of religion in our country. If, for example, one's beliefs do not allow for blood transfusions, health care providers may obtain a court order to prevent one's imposing this belief on a minor child. Similarly, if one's beliefs do not allow for the payment of taxes, generally or selectively, this tenet will be made to yield to government's need for funds. Nor will a mother be upheld in her belief that she can keep evil spirits out of her child by feeding it only salt water. On the other hand, as noted, responsible, hard-working people whose beliefs underpin a lifeworld in which only an elementary level education is deemed necessary, a state's requirement for more has been found to violate free exercise.

In short, our laws usually manage to respect and protect reasonable beliefs. What counts as reasonable depends on a mix of considerations, some more important than others in a given instance. But the dominant consideration over the years has been whether or not the beliefs in question are likely to be harmful to others or, a fortiori, to the state itself. Relevant in this regard is the familiar appeal to the threat of a clear and present danger. But a set of beliefs thought at one time to be just that might not be so considered at another time. Examples that come immediately to mind include Mormonism, Communism, and fundamentalist attitudes about alcoholic beverages. And now, because our country has experienced mass murders of innocent people, our tripartite government is struggling over new questions about what legal rights if any a dedicated terrorist should have however dangerous he or she might be to the public at large.

These various aspects of one's right to believe are dealt with differently in constitutional law depending on whether the predominant issue is free exercise or non-establishment or, alternatively, freedom of assembly or even freedom of the press. The first two clauses have historically been limited to beliefs deemed to be religious. Yet even these clauses have had a wider meaning since the Supreme Court recognized that non-religious beliefs also deserve First Amendment protection if they fulfill for a given individual a function comparable to that of religious beliefs. The key case in this regard actually involved interpretation of the federal statute authorizing conscientious objection. But the reasoning seems applicable to First Amendment "religion" cases. And indeed the Supreme Court has long held in a variety of different cases that the First Amendment requires government to be neutral not only in its dealings with different religious denominations but also as between religious and non-religious persons.

As interpreted in our courts, then, the First Amendment affords a wide range of protection to beliefs and the expression of those beliefs to others. But such protection does not legitimize harming others. And yet even this limitation is not uniformly applied. Freedom of speech is interpreted as covering advertising ("commercial speech") to the point that a service that is offered in one state but illegal in another may be advertised in the state where it is illegal. Moreover, if harm is done to a public figure (for example, a well-known politician) by publication of false information, such publication may be found libelous only if it is also shown that the publication was done maliciously or with knowledge that it was false. Freedom of the press is not so absolute, though, that a judge may not ban representatives of the news media from a courtroom if he or she deems such exclusion necessary to assure that a defendant receives a fair trial. And, what is perhaps the best known example of First Amendment law, one's right to free speech does not extend to shouting "Fire!" counterfactually in a crowded theater. Nor would the courts second-guess one's arrest under the freedom of speech clause if the evidence shows one was inciting a mob to riot.

In other words, where competing rights are at stake, the verbal absolutivity of the First Amendment yields to the complexity of actions. Limits are set to prevent a harm deemed greater than the mere infringement of one's right to believe and to express one's beliefs to others. This balancing of competing rights also applies with regard to freedom of assembly, but again not in a simple or straightforward way. In fact, no First Amendment right has been more subject to containment than freedom of assembly. In particular, organizations thought of as leftist, and hence likely to be opposed to the existing government, are given less leeway for getting together than are organizations more to the right on the political spectrum. Compare, for example, the long history of government harassment of the American Communist and American Socialist parties with the careful protection given to the American Nazi Party's right to parade in Skokie, Illinois, in spite of the emotional damage such a march would have had on Holocaust survivors living in Skokie.

Arguably, a threat of imminent danger is the controlling factor in these cases, with all the room that leaves for carefully worded panic reactions. Thus the State of Alabama's effort to obtain the membership list of the National Association for the Advancement of Colored People (NAACP) was disallowed, in part because of that organization's commitment to nonviolence. But during World War II the U.S. Supreme Court endorsed the federal government's policy of rounding up U.S. citizens of Japanese ancestry residing in California and holding them in guarded camps. Various "suspect" organizations have been subject to surveillance and infiltration by law enforcement agents, with or without court approval.

In short, there is ample precedent in this country for government intrusion in spite of the constitutional right to assemble freely. Moreover, such intrusions are usually upheld by the courts so long as it can be shown that some perceived clear and present danger was a crucial motivation. What courts seldom do, however, is determine that the government is creating the clearest and most present danger. Even if they do not, the issue at hand might be momentous enough to persuade some citizens that they have not only the right but even the duty (according to the Declaration of Independence) to change their government. This state of affairs existed in the heyday of slavery, for example, and contributed to the War Between the States. It has also been generated by issues as diverse as the income tax and "socialized medicine" or, in more contemporary terms, health care reform. But it has most often arisen in connection with a morally questionable war. To pacify the individual pacifist, the government has made allowances for a religion-inspired conscientious objector. But prison has been the instrument of pacification for many who expressed objections publicly, as a group, to an ongoing military engagement.

These are serious issues. They go to the core of why we have a government in the first place. Usually, as we have seen in this chapter, government interferes with beliefs only when the beliefs in question endanger others who are entitled to protection. Sometimes, though, the government may find certain beliefs problematic because they are perceived to endanger the government itself. This at one time determined how the US government dealt with Communists. To generalize from that example, what we have here is a case of beliefs that conflict directly with the government's own preferred beliefs. This happens if the government has what some scholars call a "civil religion" which it vigorously defends for its own sake apart from any question of fairness among equals. For details, turn the page and we'll start a new chapter.

Chapter 3
The Hidden Dangers of Civil Religion

On paper, as we have seen, a group of people who enjoy freedom of religion may believe whatever they choose. This does not mean, though, that they are free to do whatever their beliefs suggest to them. After all, what they want to do might be harmful to others who may or may not share their beliefs. So even in a democracy a government may be required to hinder some beliefs selectively. But how is this selection to be carried out? If the targeted believers really do threaten the peace in a serious way, then arguably they should be suppressed for the sake of domestic tranquility regardless of their prima facie right to assemble. Sometimes, though, even holders of beliefs that have not resulted in any action may be suppressed just the same. These beliefs, in turn, might involve not the efficacy of grace, say, but certain government policies they deem unfair or unjust. This by no means rare occurrence in which a government suppresses political beliefs is typified by the Burmese government's longstanding solitary confinement of opposition leader Aung San Suu Kyi. In such a case the suppression is based not on a finding of heresy but on a strategic decision that the beliefs in question are incompatible with the government's civil religion. As often as not these days, that religion is built around the concept of secularism. Secularism, in turn, has been liberalism's answer to pluralism.

People in the United States and most other developed countries live in a pluralist society that is subject to more or less democratic principles of government. No democracy has been pre-designed, though, to accommodate pluralism. So scholars have tried to provide rules according to which the voices of groups with diverse worldviews can be heard in the public arena. The scholars most devoted to this project are liberals, that is, they are devoted to the idea of maximizing people's freedom within reasonable limits. This project may accordingly be called the liberal policing project. Alas, this project has failed because, as already discussed, its pro-neutrality stance accommodates a bias against the public airing of any views that challenge secular dominance. It is also dangerous, because its pseudo-neutrality authorizes prior censorship and encourages acquiescence in any abuse of power that is legitimized as being on the side of reason or a fortiori science. In what follows I'll address first the failure of and then the danger inherent in secularism.

The liberal project has failed, first of all, because it is not neutral. To be sure, it calls for government neutrality as to religious preferences; but this, in effect, is an endorsement of public secularism. The liberal project also fails because it is itself ideologically driven. Its proponents persuade one another that the privatization of religion is based on considerations that somehow emanate from a neutral standpoint which is rational by definition. Identifying their own views with this neutral standpoint, they assume that this empowers them to assess the political propriety of allegedly less rational views.

This behavior involves presumptive righteousness, which is itself based on a belief system. It requires of a scholar dedicated to its cause what David Reidy (referring to Rawls) calls "rational faith" (1999: 103, 109). A scholar so dedicated in the United States often looks to the Constitution for guidance as those more religiously oriented might look to the Bible. Some analysts call this religion-like behavior "civil religion," the fundamentalist version of which is what Sanford Levinson calls "Constitutional faith" (1988).

In other words, secularists act out of their worldview in ways comparable to those displayed by any adherent of an unprovable doctrine taken on faith to be true (Bellah 1992; Lazare 1996). In this instance, the unexamined belief is in the power of reason to solve all problems. What those committed to this belief overlook is how readily it can be used to support policies and practices that are unjustly harmful to innocent people.

As a model for limiting government intrusions into people's lives, secular neutrality certainly merits attention. But as applied in actual political contexts, it may serve to limit public debate to supportive variations on the beliefs of those in power.

For, they may use it as a convenient justification for controlling public utterances in ways that range from slanted press releases to forcible suppression of disagreement. Arguably, these abuses of power are not required by the neutrality model, and might even be contrary to its proponents' intentions. But neutralists do expect political authorities to decide about and defend what they deem to be reasonable. So they have no principled basis for objecting when those whose views are found wanting in this respect are censored or otherwise constrained.

Consider first a rhetorical constraint built into the secular liberal model of neutrality. As neutralists look to logic and analysis for rules of political acceptability, they tend to disdain less rigorous kinds of argument. But these in context may be persuasive to a group of voters, jurists, elected representatives, or committee members, especially if put forward by the party in power. For, the powerful often need little genuine evidence to be persuasive. This can be seen, unfortunately, in criminal trials of defendants too poor to employ counsel in their behalf. It could be seen on an even grander scale during the Cold War as powerful interests appealed successfully to missile gaps, throwpower advantage, and megadeaths to justify their appropriations-plus-earmarks requests. Such rhetorical devices are neither definitive nor even rational, but they were taken seriously and funding followed.

These observations imply that the powerful often rely on faulty reasoning to have their way. So is it really fair, pragmatically speaking, to require defenders of a worthy cause to make sure their arguments are formulated with canonical precision? For example, might not a group of people seek a ban on cigarette smoking on the basis of less than the best medical reasons -- for example, because God prefers that we not ruin the temple that is our body? These are not at all flippant questions, as can be seen from a closer examination of how decisions are actually made in the public forum.

Electoral niceties aside, those in positions of power pay little heed to reasoning as espoused by academics. The ability of the former to control public decision making in the legislative process is well known. So I will focus here on administrative and judicial institutions, which liberals such as Rawls look to as bastions of public reasoning. And at the outset a qualification is in order. Secularists themselves no longer trust reasoning as completely as their Enlightenment predecessors did; so they cannot have unbridled confidence even in decisions that are supposedly based on reasons deemed rational as formulated and presented.

How should these reasons be understood now that absolute scientific certitude (*episteme*) has been left to the history of ideas while researchers content themselves with finding a more adequate account of assembled data (*doxa*)? This is no esoteric question of interest only to philosophers of science. For, the modernist view of scientific reasoning still helps vested interests fend off critics by denying the adequacy of their evidence. The game is actually fairly simple to play: a defender of the status quo opposes change on the grounds that reasons asserted for changing are not definitive.

An appeal to scientific reasoning is often used in debates over public policy to deny the adequacy or even the existence of evidence for the reformist position. This approach was at one time used to justify religious interference with science, as in the Galileo case. This case, on one level, involved old science in opposition to new science, or what Thomas S. Kuhn called a paradigm shift. And in fact Church leaders who were partial to the older theory did not ask Galileo to deny his astronomical findings but only to acknowledge that they lacked definitive and absolute truth. Given the absolutist view of science current in his day, he could not do this.

Today philosophers of science still seek criteria whereby to separate science from non-science (known as the demarcation problem). Most practicing scientists, meanwhile, are keenly aware of the merely incremental reliability of any scientific findings. And spokespersons for commerce and industry often draw on a kind of demarcation to immunize their charges against liability for their effects on the world. And they usually do so in the same way as did the medieval Church: posit an absolute (and unrealistic) standard of science of which available data falls short. This strategy takes several forms. One is to poison the well, that is, challenge the expertise of anyone who cites troublesome data. Another is to discredit data presented by denying it outright or, as a fallback, denying its probative value.

Undermining expertise is a convenient way to neutralize challenges to established ways of doing things, at least in the short run. As Kuhn argued, it is to be expected if a particular view of things has become institutionally entrenched, as was Ptolemaic astronomy at the time of Galileo. Centuries later Sigmund Freud was opposed by the Viennese medical establishment, as was Ignace Semmelweis, who determined empirically that puerperal fever was being transmitted to birthing mothers by doctors who went directly from dissecting cadavers to delivering babies without first washing their hands. Such individual efforts have since given way to systematically organized challenges. If these are sufficiently comprehensive, even established science policy can be reversed if its negative consequences can be shown scientifically to far outweigh benefits. An excellent illustration of this is the campaign in the 1960s to have DDT banned, first in Wisconsin and then on a national level (Loucks 1971, 1972).

Outright denial is effective against complainants too poor to do extensive discovery. Against such opposition a company or industry can defend its market position by denying liability for any alleged harm attributed to it. This strategy was adopted by companies seeking to avoid a ban on hydro fluorocarbons when scientists began blaming it for a hole in the ozone layer that increased our risk of skin cancer. It has also been the strategy of companies that seek to avoid liability or at least delay assessment of penalties by denying any causal connection between storm damage or defective medical devices or oil spills and their legal responsibilities. Should discovery eventually yield evidence of a damning link, a corporate defendant can still deny the adequacy of that evidence as grounds for requiring it to change in any way. Thus a company that at first resorts to blanket denial may later move to some such fallback position as evidence accumulates with regard to the effects of smoking tobacco, or of being exposed to Agent Orange in Vietnam or to toxic waste around Ground Zero in New York City. The obstacles against bringing a defendant from that point to a finding of liability is extremely difficult, though, as can be seen in

Jonathan Harr's account (1995) of a nine-year effort to link incidences of leukemia in Woburn, Massachusetts, to industry-discharged toxic chemicals in the water supply.

As these examples indicate, institutionalized neutrality should not be so taken for granted that its self-appointed operatives enjoy an evidentiary advantage over their critics. For, especially when clothed in the mantle of science-based discourse, an untested attribution of epistemic superiority can lead to dire consequences. This is especially the case when police or military interests don this mantle to trump values vital to a civilized culture. This often occurs when a religious group is labeled a cult and pseudo-scientific anti-cultists drown out the advice of others who are knowledgeable about the group's religious heritage. The effects of scientism are, however, even more overwhelming when applied to military endeavors.

Mythology and spin control notwithstanding, military endeavors involve a systematic process of disuniting body parts and lifeblood from their human totalities, often to the accompaniment of cacophonous sound and overpowering stench (Hedges 2002; Fussell 1989). The side whose forces do more of this unto the others or perhaps are more able to tolerate having it done unto them are declared by historians to have won, at least in the short run. Ribbons, medals, parades, and fictional re-enactments of conflicts remote in time cosmetically distract attention from the physical and mental cost of the conflict borne in the broken bodies and lives of survivors. Before the fact, those developing the weaponry for the next encounter rely on technical language to express ever so abstractly the killing efficiency to which their efforts are directed; and anyone so ill-mannered as to translate such discourse into flesh-and-blood casualty estimates is ignored as incapable of comprehending technical complexity. This pseudo-neutral rationalism was raised to new heights during the Cold War quest for nuclear weapons mastery, when the very idea of disarmament was dismissed by both technical and diplomatic experts as a naive failure to grasp the eternal verities of global confrontation (Cohn 1987).

This ability to contemplate killing only with regard to its technical aspects is very much the prerogative of males. So it is of some interest that the techno-language of killing is, on another layer, sexual in its portrayal of both male conquest through and male mothering of weapons, especially missiles. World peace would hardly be guaranteed, of course, just by bringing women's virtues to bear on weapons policy and practice. For, women too can be violent; and many feminists contend that it demeans women to deny them the opportunity to participate in front-line military action. So I grant that neither sex has a monopoly on rage or on military capabilities. Women, however, in part because of their traditional role as nurturers, are more likely to be sensitive to the impact of hostilities on real human beings (Reardon 1985). To ignore their insights, then, in the name of some superior neutral stance is in effect to equate abstract thinking with objectivity, when in fact it is only a socially approved way to put one's head in the sand.

Secularism in practice, then, is anything but neutral. It is a worldview that its adherents think of as being science-based. What is more, some even attribute revelatory significance to science. Indeed, some have declared that science offers people what religion no longer can, namely, a basis for belief. And some people are attracted to religion only if it is scientific – which may explain the special appeal of religions that claim scientific validity. This is the case, for example, with both Christian Science and Scientology. Christian Science claims to be primarily a religion that improves people's health without relying on standard medical science, so opens itself to the charge that it is irrational (DesAutels et al. 1999). The Church of Scientology, by contrast, officially declares itself to be both religious and scientific. This allows Scientologists to benefit from both labels. So opponents attack them on a third ground, namely, that they are after people's money (as if no real scientist or approved religionist would ever do such a thing). And thus is the troublesome history of selective abuse of heretics and blasphemers being relived in our day with a focus on economics. Karl Marx would endorse this project if only it were not selective in its application.

Marx, of course, called religion the opiate of the masses and expected it to become extinct once the secular paradise of Communism was established. But a consumer of an opiate needs a source, a provider; and there are good reasons why government might play that role prior to the millennium. For, according to Max Weber (no communist he), elites can be counted on to prop up religions in which they do not believe but which conveniently encourage docility in the masses. Ironically enough, the now defunct government of the Soviet Union instantiated both observations about religion, but in a vicious, destructive way neither secular prophet could have anticipated. Following Marx, the Soviet leaders first sought to extirpate traditional religion from people's consciousness; then, during World War II, they reversed this strategy enough to gain to gain the churches' financial support (Burleigh 2007, 234-237). In each instance, nonetheless, they perpetrated precisely the kind of elitist manipulation that had caught Weber's attention.

Now that the Cold War has ended, mandatory secularism is somewhat in decline, as countries no longer under the Soviet yoke, including Russia, have reinstated religious freedom and traditional religious practices are resurfacing. But the military-based secular state is unfortunately still ensconced in such religion-oppressing regimes as China, Pakistan, Myanmar, Eritrea, and Syria. In each of these countries, the government has faced tensions that invite greater openness to religious beliefs and practices. Few liberal theorists, though, have come to terms with this reality, focused as they are on preventing religion from exercising any influence on the state. Along these lines, it makes sense that UK academics would contemplate boycotting academic institutions in Israel, seeing how this state privileges one religious minority while persecuting another. Generally speaking, though, liberals just find it hard to defend people's right to protest injustice. This was apparent, for example, in the convoluted ways in which they tried to circumscribe people's right to protest the War in Vietnam.

To his credit, John Rawls wrote at the time that "if legitimate civil disobedience seems to threaten civil peace, the responsibility falls not so much on those who protest as upon those whose abuse of authority and power justifies such opposition" (1969: 255). Other scholars were no less forthright, e.g., linguist Noam Chomsky, philosopher Richard Wasserstrom, and theologian Reinhold Niebuhr. But Sidney Hook, who abandoned liberalism, articulated the mainstream liberal position in declaring civil disobedience justifiable "only when the action is sustained by a great moral principle implicit in the democratic process, and only when there is no great danger it will be a preface to riot and civil war, or imperil the functioning of democratic political life" (1970: 124-125). Hook came to this view because as an emigré survivor of unbounded civil disturbances in Europe, he saw more of the same in such events as the police riot at the 1968 Democratic Party convention. He remained blind to how minuscule was the harm done by anti-war protesters compared to the hundreds of people being killed every day to advance "American interests."

Most liberal analysts of civil disobedience during the Vietnam era agreed that whatever public position one took had to be rational or at least reasonable. They recognized, as did the American government, that an antiwar stance might be based on religious principles. But they held the line against "unreasonable" religious motivation. University of Michigan law professor Carl Cohen granted, for example, that a "higher law justification" of civil disobedience might be theological or non-theological. But he warned that the theological variety faces grave epistemological difficulties because (he said) it can't be proved (1971:105-120).

Cohen's rationalist preferences were countered by Richard Rorty's insightful observation that rationalists have epistemological problems of their own (1979: 179-180). But Rorty might have added that philosophers are not alone in this regard. Scientists in the nineteenth century still subscribed to the epistemological absolutism of Galileo and Laplace, and they had no truck with religionists who presented religion as an alternative world view. Many interbellum twentieth-century philosophers, including the logical positivists, actually sought to reduce philosophy to science. Phenomenologists meanwhile thought philosophy still had a certain cultural importance but in their own way they too aped the rigors of scientific method. A technocracy gone mad would, however, leave great scars on the first half of the twentieth century. And in response a number of academics began to recognize that the secularist dismissal of religion leaves a gap to be filled, at least with regard to normative considerations.

This openness to normative relevance is now accepted in many quarters, thereby giving religion more breathing room. But few liberals are willing to locate this room in the public sphere. Philosophers in particular have taken their cue from the positivists in this regard even as the "objective" watchtower from which they guard the secular fortress is crumbling beneath their feet. As long as it still stands, though, science-oriented secularism remains perhaps the most dangerous ideology ever concocted by our endangered species. For this reason alone, if no other, public room must be found for competing worldviews whose missions are not destructive but ameliorative. Until this becomes accepted practice, ethicists who think about these matters might reflect on the casuistry developed by scholastic moral theologians five hundred years ago.

The scholastic theologians sought to facilitate a confessor's counseling role by providing him with heuristic models with which to assess moral decisions under conditions of uncertainty. Models on offer included probabilism, equiprobabilism, and probabiliorism. They were intended to help guide penitents to sin-free decisions, provided that what someone wants to do is, respectively, probably ethical, no less probably ethical, or more probably so, than doing otherwise. Probably ethical meant at least one learned authority says so; no less probably ethical, authorities are about equally divided on the question; and more probably ethical, more authorities are supportive than not.

This old system is hardly a panacea for resolving the complex issues generated by the results of scientific research. But it does tell us that even if experts agree about the facts and even about the theory used to explain them, they may not agree about acceptable applications. To remain "sinless" under these circumstances, no decision procedure should be applied that depends on limited and perhaps self-interested expertise. There may be no such disinterested decision maker. But we have long been led to believe that our courts embody this standard as well as can be expected. So let's turn now to an examination of just how well our courts do manage to treat religion in a neutral way.

PART II
STATE/RELIGION BORDER CONTROL

We've seen how theorists have dealt with the problem (as they see it) of keeping religion from intruding too much into affairs of state. They don't all agree, of course, as to how much would be too much. But most are persuaded that a secularist slant is best suited for avoiding conflicts in a pluralist society. Whether this is the case or not is a matter of some dispute. And it just so happens that disputes have a tendency to wind up in courts, which thus take on the task of maintaining a kind of border control between state and religion. This is especially so in the United States.

In European countries separation of state and religion is now firmly entrenched in the workings of society (Rémond 1999). And in the United States secularists consider separation of state and religion the only legitimate position allowed under the First Amendment to the Constitution. In reality, though, neither elected officials nor courts accept this dichotomy without modification. The former use religion for all sorts of strategic objectives (Domke and Coe 2008), notably to generate support for military endeavors. The latter have not faulted these major forms of intermingling; but they have sought to keep schools free of proselytizers. Lately, however, the U.S. Supreme Court has been shifting from so-called separationist to accommodationist interpretations of the religion clauses, first with regard to education and more recently with regard to other faith-based endeavors (Rosen 2000).

In other words, after a long period of time during which the Court handed down close to unanimous decisions upholding strict separation, it began issuing 5-4 decisions that accommodate religion in some way. And so long as this majority is maintained, still other accommodating decisions are likely. To show this change in attitude on the Court I will review in Chapter 4 some of its major holdings with regard to religion, especially in education-related cases. In Chapter 5 I will provide a brief history of how religious groups have responded to the education-related rulings. My focus will be on how American Catholics first developed a parochial school system in response to the separationist stance and now are rethinking this commitment in light of the Court's accommodationist shift. I will also address the response of other religious groups.

Chapter 4

Religion-State Relations in U.S. Courts

Early on I noted that the basic rule regarding religion-state relations in the United States is located in the First Amendment to the Constitution, which contains (among other things) two clauses regarding how state and religion are to get along. The so-called non-establishment clause prohibits there being an established religion in this country. The so-called free exercise clause prohibits the state from intruding without just cause in the affairs of a legitimate religion.

Courts in the United States have interpreted nonestablishment and free exercise of religion in numerous concrete circumstances and in response to almost opposite kinds of concerns. Nonestablishment cases tend to be brought by secularists opposed to what they consider unfair advantages enjoyed by religious organizations, notably tax exemption and/or direct government subsidies used for religious purposes. A free exercise case is likely to be brought by a religious organization that is challenging government interference in what it claims to be constitutionally protected activities. In earlier times the courts interpreted each clause somewhat narrowly, favoring government prerogatives over those of religion. This, however, has begun to change in both kinds of cases.

It is not possible to cover the wide range of issues that are addressed in light of the First Amendment religion-related clauses. But within the space allotted I'll first consider the two clauses in order -- first free exercise cases, then those that concern nonestablishment – then I will focus on how these clauses have been applied specifically to education.

Rulings Concerning Religion-State Relations

In assessing the scope of free exercise, U.S. courts tend to respect long established religious assemblages more than those that have emerged more recently and are accordingly less predictable. But they have at times applied the free exercise clause to protect a group with more anomalous beliefs and practices, especially if they saw no principled way to disfavor such a group without providing a precedent for attacking major religions as well. If they uphold government interference, it is likely to be on the basis of its responsibility for maintaining public safety and good order; but this result is reached less often today than a century ago. This can be seen from the following rulings.

In 1878 the U.S. Supreme Court upheld a Utah law that forbade Mormons to practice polygamy (*Reynolds v. U.S.*). Sixty years later, though, in a series of cases involving the Jehovah's Witnesses the Court made state laws on religion subject to U.S. constitutional law. In 1938, it ruled 8-0 that an individual Jehovah's Witness had a freedom of the press right to distribute pamphlets: *Lovell v. City of Griffin* (303 U.S. 444. Then in 1940 a 9-0 Court for the first time applied the free exercise clause to the states in another Jehovah's Witness pamphlet distribution case: *Cantwell v. Connecticut* (310 U.S. 296, 1940). But a year later in *Cox v. New Hampshire* (312 U.S. 569) it held that for reasons of safety and order Jehovah's Witnesses are subject to parade permit legislation. Then in 1947 in *Everson v. Board of Education of Ewing* (330 U.S. 1) it for the first time applied both religion clauses to the states.

Such protection of religious activities is more to be expected if the Court finds that the group's beliefs and/or practices are close to the mainstream or contribute to the public good or if singled out for special accommodation would set an awkward precedent. Thus in the 1880s it saw no precedent-setting problem in upholding Utah's denial of the vote to Mormons whether they practiced polygamy or not. For, it reasoned, acceptance of the underlying belief amounts to acquiescence in others' committing polygamy (*Davis v. Beason*, 133 U.S. 333, 345). A century later it avoided precedent setting by striking down a Minnesota law that singled out the Unification Church for special financial scrutiny, and it refused to exempt Amish employers from paying social security taxes. In 1990 the Court chose not to defend

Native Americans in Oregon who were fired and denied unemployment benefits because they use state-prohibited peyote in their religious rites. Congress then passed the Religious Freedom Restoration Act of 1993 (RFRA) to protect such practices. That same year the Court invalidated a city ordinance that proscribed animal sacrifice as practiced by a group of immigrants in Florida: *Church of the Lukumi Babalu Aye Inc. v. Hialeah,* 508 U.S. 520.

These cases show that the task of finding a principled limit to accommodation is an ongoing challenge to the Court. Consider in this regard a 1944 decision best known for a dissenting opinion. The Court in a 5-4 decision ruled against postal authorities' applying a mail fraud statute to a religious group promising to cure incurable illnesses. Dissenting, Justice Robert H. Jackson faulted the Court for even addressing the merits of the case. For, he argued, however much "mental and spiritual poison (the victims of false prophets) get," "that is precisely the thing the Constitution puts beyond the reach of the prosecutor, for the price of freedom of religion . . . is that we must put up with, and even pay for, a good deal of rubbish" (*U.S. v. Ballard,* 322 U.S. 78, 95).

Justice Jackson's hands-off stance has had a mixed progeny. The Court fine-tuned it in *Thomas v. Review Board* (450 U.S. 707, 1981), by saying that to merit First Amendment protection a group's religious beliefs "need not be acceptable, logical, consistent or comprehensible to others" nor do its practices (short of non-spiritual threats or coercion) need to be widely recognized as appropriate and commendable. Think about it, though. Doesn't the principled tolerance here called for assume that courts are competent to decide whether a religious practice does or does not merit protection against government intrusion? How otherwise could it support the Church of Wicca's "white" as opposed to others' "black" witchcraft. Experts in these matters might be helpful, but identifying appropriate experts is itself problematic. This was apparent when government agencies turned to such self-styled experts as the Cult Awareness Network, the American Family Foundation, and the Council of Mind Abuse to guide their policy towards the Branch Davidians (Tabor and Gallagher, 1995).

Non-establishment is also a basic constitutional principle, but its import has been difficult to pinpoint in particular cases. There has never been an established church in the United States at the federal level, but in 1892 Justice David Brewer wrote for the majority in *Holy Trinity v. U.S.* that the United States is a Christian country. This attitude has found expression in a number of rulings, especially where moral standards are at issue. Such rulings, however, are routinely justified on secular grounds. This is true, for example, of decisions that upheld the constitutionality of Sunday closing laws and, of even greater import, approved granting property-tax exemption to religious organizations: *McGowan v. Maryland* (1961) [366 U.S. 420] and *Waltz v. Tax Commission of City of New York* (1970)[397 U.S. 664], respectively.

In 1971, the U.S. Supreme Court set forth something of a lodestone for limiting state accommodation of religion. A law, it ruled 7-0, is constitutional if it has a secular purpose, a primary effect that neither advances nor inhibits religion, and no excessive entanglement between religion and state: *Lemon v. Kurtzmann*, 403 U.S. 602. In this case, discussed below, excessive entanglement was found. Likewise later in *Kiryas Joel Board of Education v. Grumet* (1994, 517 U.S. 687) a 6-3 majority required the State of New York to modify its support of a Hasidic Jewish community's educational arrangements for disabled youth because these advanced a religious as well as a secular purpose. Then in 1997 the Court issued a ruling that some commentators say gives nonestablishment higher priority than free exercise (NYT 6/26-27/1997; Hamilton 2007: ch. 8). Perhaps. But the Court did have other fish to fry.

In *City of Boerne,Texas v. Flores* (1997, 521 U.S. 507), a 6-3 majority used a zoning dispute to strike down RFRA as too accommodating and, what is worse, disrespectful of both local government and the Court's authority. The narrow issue in this case was whether a municipal government had the authority to include a church in an historic preservation zone and on that basis deny a bishop's application for a building permit. The broader issue, though, was whether Congress had the power to add substantive content to the Fourteenth Amendment. The Rehnquist court, then on a campaign to build up states' rights, sacrificed Archbishop Flores to that cause. (Four years later a 5-4 court also disappointed disabled individuals seeking damages from their state university employer under the Americans With Disabilities Act: *Board of Trustees of the University of Alabama v. Garrett*, 531 U.S. 356.)

Earlier cases involving religious symbols or closing laws went back and forth trying to locate the point at which government accommodation of religion crosses the line to unconstitutional entanglement. A creche as one part of a mostly secular Christmas display passed muster 5-4 in *Lynch v. Donnelly* (1984, 465 U.S. 668). Five years later the Court voted 5-4 against allowing an unaccompanied creche in a court house and 6-3 in support of a Jewish menorah outside a city building: *Allegheny County v. ACLU*, 1989, 492 U.S. 573.

The lack of clear principle underlying these rulings is also evident in cases that address Sunday closing laws. In four cases decided in 1961 the Court authorized such laws as being secular in intent and supportive of religion only indirectly. In 1963 it struck down a Sunday closing statute for hindering a Seventh-Day Adventist's free exercise (*Sherbert v. Verner*, 374 U.S. 398); then in 1985 it invalidated a statute that authorized employees to pick their own day of rest: *Thornton v. Caldor, Inc.*, 472 U.S. 703.

The complexity of accommodation is especially apparent in cases having to do with opposition to and refusal to fight in wars. In these matters the courts have been sensitive to the needs of the military for personnel and support, yet they have recognized first religious and then secular convictions to the contrary. In so doing they have established bases for both civil disobedience (considered above) and conscientious objection. The latter in particular grew in importance as conscription became an accepted way to prosecute a war. It was utilized but not tested in the courts during the Civil War, received U.S. Supreme Court endorsement during World War I, and continued uncontested until the Vietnam War, following which it was eliminated, except for a registration requirement. In the interim, an exception was made for conscientious objection.

This exception for conscientious objection began as a narrow accommodation for pacifists but had to be expanded as the Court found no other way to defend it against challenges based on the First Amendment religion clauses. In *Selective Draft Law Cases* (1918, 245 U.S. 366), the Court unanimously rejected establishment claims that pacifist religions were being favored by the 1917 Draft Act, which exempted from combat only members of a "well-recognized religious sect or organization" whose creed forbade "members to participate in war in any form." This language endured in subsequent draft law enactments but without singling out pacifists. According to the Military Selective Service Act of 1967 [50 U.S.C. App. Sec. 456(j)], a successful petitioner had to be "by reason of religious training and belief, conscientiously opposed to participation in war in any form.". Recognizing the strength of the establishment claim challenging this law, the Court in *United States v. Seeger* (1965, 380 U.S. 163) and *Welsh v. United States* (1970, 398 U.S. 333) simply redefined religion to include any moral and philosophical tenets held with the strength of traditional religious convictions. Faced, however, with a petitioner opposed to a particular war on the basis of his (Catholic) church's teachings about just war standards, the Court chose to see no selective establishment lest it invite selective compliance with law: *Gillette v. United States* (1970, 401 U.S. 437).

The kinds of issues addressed in these cases also came up for consideration, with context-specific nuances, with regard to state-religion relations in schools. Prima facie, one would think the outcome of a religious rights case should be the same whether it involves fighting a war or educating students. And up to a point this is what happens, in that both kinds of cases enlist the Court as arbiter of secular neutrality. There are differences, however, in that K-12 school cases, such as *Lemon* and *Kiryas Joel*, involve institutions that educate minors. Minors in a private school are at a disadvantage because their school may be less well funded than are public schools as it seeks to provide an adequate education. Minors in a public school may be subjected to and yet be comparatively defenseless against unwanted indoctrination. So schools have become a focal point for debating both free exercise and nonestablishment of religion in the United States.

For the most part, the Court has remained rigorous in its education-related rulings when the issue before it involves the constitutional need to keep both public schools and the state neutral regarding religious preferences. A comparable rigor has prevailed regarding how much if at all the state may aid religion-based schools. There have been changes, though, because of major shifts in the demographic mix of religious groups and which groups choose to maintain their own schools. In the nineteenth century, first Protestantism and then secularism prevailed in the public schools; and various religious groups, especially Catholics, opted out in favor of maintaining their own schools. In the twentieth century, a bland mixture of secularism and civic ideals offered a more accommodating atmosphere for most varieties of Christian belief. Now in the twenty-first century, the growing presence of non-Christian believers, including Muslims, is opening a new phase of state-religion relations as to education. All this is the focus of Chapter 5. Here the focus is on the role of the courts in setting the constitutional parameters.

Rulings on Religion-State Relations in Education

Liberal states are theoretically divided into a public sphere in which reason alone has voice and a private sphere in which religions, among other things, can be tolerated. This dichotomy is easy enough to express with clarity. But locating it with precision within a particular institution requires considerable nuance. This is especially so with regard to educational institutions. For example, where secularism is enshrined in legislated government policy, e.g., in Turkey and France, the seemingly humble act of wearing a traditional Muslim headscarf (*khimar*) in school has been the subject of politically heated constitutional battles. This particular challenge to secularism is not yet as heated an issue in American public schools. But these schools have been at the center of their own idiosyncratic controversies about what sort of interaction between secularism and religion may be tolerated.

A century ago separationism was bolstered by the idea of a melting pot, in that this threat of amalgamation inspired religious groups to maintain traditional integrity by practicing unobtrusive noncompliance. They have since become more demanding, though, and the courts sometimes accommodate their preferences. The significance of this change will be illustrated by reviewing how Catholics responded to separationism by developing schools in their parishes and service organizations in secular colleges and universities. To understand this historical process, however, one must be aware of how separationism was being interpreted in public discourse and in law.

The ties between religion and education in the United States have a long and varied history. In colonial days and for decades thereafter all schools on all levels were church-affiliated. After the Civil War secular schools were founded anew or emerged out of religion-based institutions. On the K-12 level public schools were established, usually with a Protestant orientation. Immigration from Catholic countries later in the nineteenth century upset the value-assumptions in the public schools; but as Protestantism remained dominant Catholics established their own schools. Secularism has since become the official standard in public schools, so many conservative Protestants and others have established their own private schools.

The public school system was originally justified as an altogether suitable instrument with which to introduce all children to the common values of this country. Dominated from the outset by Protestant presumptions, this objective in time became the bastion for opposing supposedly un-American values that second-wave immigrants espoused. This led to two cases in the 1920s in which the U.S. Supreme Court struck down overzealous efforts to mandate educational uniformity. In *Meyer v. Nebraska* (1923, 262 U.S. 390), the Court ruled 7-2 that the Fourteenth Amendment guarantee of liberty precluded a state requirement that all instruction through eighth grade be in English. Two years later in *Peirce v. Society of Sisters* (288 U.S. 510) it voted unanimously against an Oregon law that required children ages 8 to 16 to attend a public school. This case in effect endorsed parallel systems of education, one that excluded and one that included religion. What remained for the Court to determine was to what extent religion could be accommodated in the public schools and secular purposes government-supported in parochial schools. Each question invites similar constitutional analysis, but the concrete issues are different and can be considered in turn.

The U.S. Supreme Court has long opposed any form of religious exercise in or under the auspices of a public school. In cases testing this position it has had to choose between a routinely replicated set of amicus briefs submitted by separationist and accommodationist interest groups; and separationism has prevailed with respect to K-12 institutions. The issues most often addressed involve religious instruction, prayer, or use of controversial readings such as the Bible or material about evolution. Take religious education as an example. An 8-1 court In *McCollum v. Board of Education* (1948, 333 U.S. 203) banned religious instruction on public school property. But a 6-3 majority in *Zorach v. Clauson* (1952, 343 U.S. 306) let a public school adjust its schedule so students could receive religious instruction off-premises.

In a series of cases the Court juridically ousted religion from the public school setting. A 7-1 majority in *Engel v. Vitale* (1962, 370 U.S. 421) rejected prayer in public schools; and an 8-1 majority in *Murray v. Curlett* and *Abington School District v. Schempp* (both 1963, 374 U.S. 203) proscribed both prayer and Bible reading in a public school. A 6-3 majority in *Wallace v. Jaffree* (1985, 472 U.S. 38) banned any officially endorsed moment of silent prayer or meditation. A mere 5-4 majority in *Lee v. Weisman* (1992, 505 U.S. 577) opposed active clergy involvement in a public school graduation ceremony; then a 6-3 majority ruled that letting student-elected chaplains say a prayer before the football team's home games violated the establishment clause: *Santa Fe Independent School District v. Doe*, 530 U.S. 290, 2000).

The teaching of evolution has generated much heat and some innovative arrangements in the K-12 curriculum. In *Epperson v. Arkansas* (1968, 393 U.S. 97) a unanimous Court found no secular justification for a statutory ban on teaching about a scientific theory. Then a 7-2 Court ruled in *Edwards v. Aguillard* (1987, 482 U.S. 578) that a Louisiana statute mandating "equal time" for creation science unconstitutionally favors a religious view. Between these two cases a 5-4 majority ruled that the Ten Commandments are not secular enough to be posted in a public school: *Stone v. Graham* (1980, 449 U.S. 39).

Parallel to these decisions keeping religion out of public schools are other decisions aimed at keeping the state out of private schools. As early as 1930, the U.S. Supreme Court announced a "child benefit" theory to endorse use of state funds to buy schoolbooks for children in parochial schools: *Cochran v. Louisiana*, 281 U.S. 370. Then in 1947 a 5-4 ruling authorized state-subsidized bus rides for children attending parochial schools, incorporated the free exercise clause into the Fourteenth Amendment, and agreed that separation of religion and state must be rigorously maintained: *Everson v Board of Education of Ewing Township* (1947, 330 U.S. 1). And so in a number of subsequent cases a majority found unconstitutional entanglement in state funding of a parochial school's field trip transportation, instructional and testing materials, payments to teachers of secular subjects, and tuition reimbursement to parents. The three latter issues have been *causes célèbres* as the Court struggled to regularize its doctrine of separation.

The doctrine of separation was defined with misguided rigor in the *Lemon v. Kurtzmann* tripartite test for constitutional separation: a secular legislative purpose, no excessive entanglement of religion and state, and a primary effect that neither advances nor hinders religion. In this case (1971, 403 U.S. 602) it ruled 7-0 that Pennsylvania and Rhode Island statutes authorizing the use of state funds to reimburse private school teachers of secular subjects violated its new test. It then found against New York's program to reimburse private schools for state mandated testing, by an 8-1 vote in *Levitt v. Community for Public Education and Religious Liberty* (1973, 413 U.S. 472) and 6-3 in *New York v. Cathedral Academy* (1977, 434 U.S. 125). It endorsed Ohio's approach to special needs testing in *Wolman v. Walter* (1977), discussed below. But it struck down programs in which both public-school and parochial-school teachers taught secular subjects on parochial school premises. It did so by a 5-4 vote in *Committee for Public Education and Religious Liberty v.*

Regan (1980, 444 U.S. 646) and a 7-2 vote in *Grand Rapids School District v. Ball* (1985, 473 U.S. 373). In *Aguilar v. Felton* (1985, 473 U.S. 402) a 5-4 majority ruled against New York City's use of federal funds to pay people who taught remedial reading and mathematics on parochial school property. For the next twelve years the city offered the courses to parochial school children in leased vans that were parked on the street.

Signs of a shift then began to appear, e.g., in a 1993 case that applied *Widmar v. Vincent* (see below) to authorize the use of K-12 school facilities to show a religious film: *Lamb's Chapel v. Center Moriches Union Free School District*, 508 U.S. 384. Then in *Agostoni v. Felton* (1997, 521 U.S. 203) a different 5-4 majority declared that *Aguilar* had in effect already been overturned, thus opening the door to a more accommodating view of the nonestablishment clause. A few years later a 6-3 majority endorsed a religious group's use of school property for meetings: *Good News Club v Milford Central School*, 533 US 98 (2001). Such holdings, moreover, would not be altogether without precedent.

As noted, the Court has upheld property-tax exemption for church property, and has at times endorsed arrangements that directly benefit the child. But the public good reasoning behind these holdings has not automatically applied to parents' parochial school expenses. In 1973, a 6-3 Court found that New York and Pennsylvania reimbursement plans failed the *Lemon* test: *Committee for Public Education and Religious Liberty v. Regan* (413 U.S. 756) and *Sloan v. Lemon* (413 U.S. 825), respectively. Ten years later, though, a 5-4 decision in *Mueller v. Allen* (463 U.S. 388) upheld a Minnesota tax deduction for tuition, books, and transportation expenses incurred for a child at any school, public, nonsectarian, or religion-related.

Subsequent sharply divided decisions have gone both ways in judging the applicability of general state assistance programs to students whose parents send them to a parochial school. A 6-3 ruling disallowed providing technical aids to parochial school students with special needs: *Meek v. Pittenger* (1975, 421 U.S. 349).

Then an 8-1 majority in *Wolman v. Walter* upheld Ohio's provision of off-premises diagnostic services to parochial school students who applied for special assistance (1977, 433 U.S. 229). A 5-4 ruling in 1993 endorsed using federal money to pay a sign-language interpreter for a deaf student in a Catholic school: *Zobrest v. Cataline Foothills School District* (509 U.S. 1); and another 5-4 ruling in 2002 allowed use of public vouchers for students' tuition at religious schools: *Zelman v. Simmons-Harris*, 536 U.S. 639.

The *Zelman* decision has inspired people in various places to establish a religion-accommodating charter school, and in each instance public controversy has ensued. Typically at issue in these instances is to prevent any use of public funds to promote religion directly, this being in violation of longstanding Court holdings. But the current Court under Chief Justice Roberts has a more nuanced view of the constitutional status of religion in K-12 schools, especially as to government assistance to private schools; and further change in juridical policy may be forthcoming. In the meantime changes have taken place regarding religion in higher education.

The rigid wall of separation has never applied to private colleges and universities. And many of these from the time of their founding by sectarian organizations and throughout the nineteenth century expected their students to participate in religious ceremonies, including compulsory chapel. Such requirements have been abolished in most major institutions but are still enforced in faith-based colleges and, ironically, at each of the three U.S. military academies (Army, Navy, and Air Force). State institutions of higher learning have honored separation much more meticulously, even as to what matters may be studied in the curriculum. In particular, a strong secular bias long prevented the introduction of courses dealing with religion. Since World War II, however, programs dedicated to the objective study of one or more religions have blossomed, and Religious Studies (or, e.g., Jewish or Islamic Studies) now has an established if not universally respected niche in most public institutions of higher learning. Meanwhile, court rulings based on equal-access considerations have helped articulate a place for religious groups on secular college campuses.

In contrast to its K-12 jurisprudence, the U.S. Supreme Court has for the most part supported accommodation at the college and university level. For example, in *Widmar v. Vincent* (1981, 454 U.S. 263) the Court ruled 8-1 that a state university could not bar a nondenominational religious group from holding services in facilities available to other student groups. In 1995 a 5-4 majority held that a state university cannot deny student activity funds to students engaged in religious activities: *Rosenberger v. Rector and Visitors of the University of Virginia*, 515 U.S. 819. In 2000, a unanimous 9-0 Court in *Board of Regents of the University of Wisconsin v. Southworth* (529 U.S. 217) upheld the university' free speech "viewpoint neutrality" practice of allocating some student fee money to student organizations whose views religious conservative students opposed.

Quite apart from these accommodations, many students affiliated with faith communities have matriculated in public colleges and universities, in spite of their parents' worries about possible challenges to their beliefs. But over time the allegedly secularist model of K-12 public school education has been losing the support of diverse community groups. The quality of the public schools, especially in inner cities, has deteriorated as funding lags, and this is giving new life to inner city Catholic schools, the majority of whose students are no longer Catholic or, for that matter, white. Minimally paid nuns have become a vanishing resource, though, so tuition must be substantial – if necessary, helped by subsidies, including perhaps vouchers in due time. The educational institutions associated with these historical processes have, in short, remained uniform in name only. Along the way, public opinion has been shifting, and the courts are beginning to read the Constitution through different glasses.

Christian fundamentalists have established schools of their own on all levels to protect their beliefs, and have gained some government support. In response to the poor quality of education in many public schools both secularist and sectarian parents have obtained controversial government support for K-12 charter schools. And most recently, especially since 11 September 2001, Muslims in the United States have been establishing private schools that substitute Islamic values for what they consider the amoral culture of public schools. In so doing, these diverse groups are in some respects repeating a process first undertaken in this country by American Catholics.

Chapter 5
Alternative Schooling in America

Growing up in Peoria, Illinois, my sister and I went to a Catholic parochial school, located just a block up the street -- this having determined our family's choice of residence. The boy next door was Protestant, so he went to the public grammar school. He also went to a public high school as I and my sister attended gender-segregated Catholic secondary schools and then did further studies in other Catholic institutions. That's the way it was for dutiful American Catholics in the twentieth century. That was our world, a world in which Catholics built schools that protected their youth from Protestantism and, worse, secularism. Along with society at large, I have outlived that ideological dichotomy. So I can now reconsider it here in light of changes in our complex pluralist arrangements, mostly for the better.

The melting pot model of integration once constituted the principal justification for supporting public schools in the United States. But over time many Americans increasingly viewed their society as being made up of largely incompatible groups. The resulting tension, in part class-based and in part religion-based, has resulted in various alternative educational institutions. I will consider several recent ones below, after focusing on their most obvious predecessor, the Catholic school system. For the record, though, there are also a number of private Protestant schools.

The earliest private schools in America were mostly Protestant; and as public schools were introduced these tended to be Protestant-dominated as well. In the next century, though, Protestantism gave way to secularism in the public schools; and court decisions solidified this arrangement. So many Protestant groups began establishing their own private schools. Christian Schools International, founded to utilize the Bible as a text in 1921, today has 100,000 students in some 500 schools. The Association of Christian Schools International, founded in 1978, now has 5300 schools enrolling 1.2 million students in some 100 countries. The Association of Classical and Christian Schools, founded in 1996, has 7800 students in 70 schools. The Seventh Day Adventists, though, serve the largest number of Protestant students: 1.3 million in 7,000 schools located in over 100 countries, including 65,000 students in 1049 schools in the US, Canada, and Bermuda.

Long before Protestants began seeking alternatives to secular public schools, American Catholics developed alternatives of their own, initially to get out from under Protestant influence. Their solution was to establish and fund schools in parishes under diocesan jurisdiction. Many of these were up and running by 1900, and the number would continue to grow for another half century. Some retrenchment is now underway but there are still some 8500 K-12 Catholic schools serving 2.7 million students. To comprehend this religious minority's faith-based building spree, let's retrace its history.

Most public schools established during our nation's first half century built a Protestant mind set into their curriculum. American Catholic bishops objected in vain, so eventually decided to develop a separate educational system for Catholic youth. The evolution of this policy can be seen in pastoral letters issued by the Provincial Councils of Baltimore (1829-1843). The first four councils did not mandate a separate education. But the Pastoral of 1833 spoke of needing to supplement children's secular learning with "a strict protection of their morals and the best safeguards of their faith." The 1837 Pastoral noted comparable problems on the college level. In the 1840 Pastoral, the bishops expressed concern about use of the King James version of the Bible and especially about a climate of hostility towards religious minorities in public schools. Catholic pupils, they contended, were being exposed Ain their tender youth to ... the mockery or the superciliousness of those who undervalue their creed." In such a setting they risked "the nearly total abandonment of their religious practices." So, the bishops concluded, Catholics would need to build schools attached to their parishes..

Even as this separationist solution was emerging, Horace Mann and others were secularizing the public schools (1837-1850). The Catholic bishops were even more displeased with secularism, though; and Pope Pius IX's encyclical on Christian education (1851) supported their concerns. So at their First Plenary Council of Baltimore (1852) they issued a pastoral letter that warned Catholic parents about "the evils of an uncatholic education" against which their children needed to be protected. After the Civil War the bishops met again at their Second Plenary Council of Baltimore (1866), and issued a pastoral letter that bemoaned the presence of Catholics in secular colleges. For, they contended, fulfilling one's duties in life is far more important than studies that are "either high or ornamental," especially if the "circumstances" of such studies are objectionable. They then followed this up with a combination of legislation and implementation.

First the bishops asked Rome for advice, and received back an "Instruction to the Bishops of the United States concerning the Public Schools" (1875). This document urged establishment of Catholic grade schools and allowed attendance at public schools only if the danger to one's faith could be neutralized and parents took responsibility for the souls of children being thus educated. At the Third Plenary Council of Baltimore (1884), the bishops endorsed these rules as the basis for "a truly Christian and Catholic education." They added as a corollary that attendance at a public school would require the explicit permission of one's bishop; and, to their credit, they cited the superior quality of the public school as a reason to grant such permission.

At the same council the bishops worried about the dangers facing Catholic students in institutions of higher learning. For, they opined, the United States was becoming a bastion of paganism. As they expressed this in a pastoral letter, the American people were succumbing to "wild theories which reject or ignore Revelation, undermine morality, and end not infrequently by banishing God from His own creation." What is worse, they said, is that the heralds of this growing unbelief "seek to mould the youthful mind in our colleges and seats of learning." Given how grave were these dangers facing Catholic undergraduates on secular campuses, the bishops needed to come up with a remedy. This remedy, some decided, would be found in persuading the laity to help pay for a university of their own in the nation's capital. It would be called The Catholic University of America. And, according to its principal proponent, John Lancaster Spalding, Bishop of Peoria, Illinois, it would be "a centre of life and light" against "false theories and systems" taught to "the sons of wealthy Catholics" in "institutions where their faith is undermined."

A significant minority of bishops did not endorse the separationist policy on which this comprehensive building project was based. For to them the idea of having all Catholic students on all levels in Catholic schools was unnecessary in some situations and futile as a general aspiration. Their assimilationist stance eventually won papal endorsement at the end of the nineteenth century. But the separationist majority of bishops persevered in their quest for a church-based K-12 school system.

This quest was successful on many fronts; but it took different forms in response to different demographics. No parochial schools seemed necessary in Pennsylvania coal towns, for example, since all the people were Catholic. In Boston, Irish Catholics eventually would control even the public school system, over half of whose pupils were Catholic by 1930. (Morris 1997: 123, 176.)

As an alternative, the moderate bishops favored the Poughkeepsie Plan, under which a local school board would lease a parochial school during regular school hours and pay nuns regular salaries to teach the public school curriculum; then after hours they would teach religion classes. Bishop Ireland implemented this plan in two towns in his Minnesota diocese and Pope Leo XIII's *Propaganda Fidei* (1892) approved it. The conservative bishops thereupon persuaded a moral theologian at Catholic University to write a pamphlet accusing the moderate bishops of being too supportive of "secular control," then asked Rome to back them.

The pope responded with a warning about "Americanism," which involved doctrines no American bishop espoused. It also declared the Baltimore decrees to be still "in full force," but left the door open to compromise experiments. Later that year, the pope sent a new delegate to the United States and he told the bishops that the Catholic Church favors the establishment of public schools that cultivate "the useful arts and the natural sciences" and encourages efforts to bring such schools into conformity with "the truths of Christianity and morality." The following May, Pope Leo XIII wrote to Cardinal Gibbons that the rules of Third Baltimore were to be "steadfastly observed." This settled policy at least on the primary level for half a century: separationist bishops built hundreds of primary schools as well as many secondary schools in urban areas, notably Philadelphia and Chicago, to accommodate some 250,000 students (Morris 1997: 99-101, 114). Meanwhile, the question of educating young Catholics on the baccalaureate level gradually emerged as an issue.

The idea that one Catholic university could provide all the higher education needs of all Catholic students is ludicrous in retrospect -- but perhaps not when first conceived. In 1890 there were only 20,000 students enrolled in all secular colleges and universities; and in 1900 the number had grown to around 45,000. This growth was already indicative of an emerging demand; but at the turn of the century only four percent of Americans aged 18-21 were enrolled in a college or university. So it was still possible for Bishop Spalding and others to believe they could have their secular cake and eat it with religious icing by opening one university for Catholic high-achievers. But a few young Catholics were already attending secular universities, and many more would follow. So the Church would need to follow its future leaders into these secularist institutions. The momentum for this shift in strategy came from an unlikely source.

In an encyclical on catechetical instruction (*Acerbo nimis*, 1905) Pope Pius X ordered all dioceses to provide "religious doctrine classes" at "public academies, colleges and universities . . . wherein no mention whatsoever is made of religion." In the United States, this had in fact already begun in a small way. In 1894, just four years after the death of Cardinal Newman in England, some health care students at the University of Pennsylvania organized a "Newman Club," to which the Roman Catholic diocese assigned a "quasi-chaplain." By 1901 there were twenty such clubs around the country. In 1907 the "Spiritual Director" for Catholics at Harvard University addressed the topic at a meeting of the fledgling National Catholic Education Association in Milwaukee, then published a study that located almost half of the 18,400 Catholic college students on secular campuses (Farrell, 1907). But the hierarchy for the most part still favored a separationist policy.

In 1917 a codified version of Canon Law came out that obligated Catholic parents to support Catholic schools (Canons 1372-83). Canon 1374 in effect universalized the 1875 Instruction to U.S. Catholic bishops: no attendance at schools "which are open also to non-Catholics" without permission of one's bishop, to be given only if "precautions against the danger of perversion" can be avoided. This mandatory isolationism targeted K-12, but American bishops applied it to attendance at colleges and universities as well. In a pastoral letter issued in 1918 they urged support for the Catholic University (where they would be meeting annually) and insisted that to counter the false doctrines taught in secular schools the Church had to have "a system of education distinct and separate from other systems." By 1926, however, though some 61-75,000 students were enrolled in Catholic institutions of higher learning, at least that many were attending state universities (out of a total of some 250,000). And the latter had to deal with a new innovation aimed at softening the impact of secularism: compulsory chapel attendance.

Chapel attendance was at the time mandatory at a number of universities, especially among those privately endowed. Debate on the merits of this requirement put the values of religious freedom and pluralism up against claims that nondenominational rites could be provided. Eventually appeals to First Amendment rights ended most mandatory attendance rules. Meanwhile, the papal Holy Office forbade Catholics to take part in any gathering that had as its aim to bring Christians together into "a religious confederation" (1927). The following year Pope Pius XI issued an encyclical (*Mortalium Animos*) that forbade Catholics to participate in any "panchristian" project that fostered relativism of dogma, modernism in theology, or indifferentism in ecclesiology. That was hardly a problem in the United States, since secularism was the dominant worldview at most universities, at least among professors. Iowa State University, though, was something of an exception.

In 1927, Iowa State incorporated a School of Religion as an integral part of the Liberal Arts College. Its mission was to offer degree-oriented courses in religion on both the undergraduate and the graduate level. The courses were to be taught by representatives of the various faiths who would be paid by their respective religious institutions. (Due to low enrollments courses on Catholic doctrine were suspended in 1931.) Meanwhile, Newman Club representatives meeting in Toronto in 1928 had defined their role primarily in terms of devotional ministry. A year later Pope Pius XI responded to Fascists' growing control of education in Italy with an encyclical (*Divini illius Magistri*) that stressed the role of family and Church in educating youth and the dangers of studying at any level in a non-Catholic school. Papal preferences notwithstanding, in 1933 there were more American Catholic students attending secular colleges and universities full time (83,000) than were enrolled in Catholic institutions (79,000).

To this quantitative failure must be added a qualitative lapse: no Catholic institution of higher learning was comparable, say, to Harvard University. Far from all American Catholics concluded from this, however, that Harvard would be a better place to matriculate. For, according to the Jesuit weekly *America* (14 March 1931), Catholic youth would be defenseless in a secular institution. For, they "have no fund of knowledge about anything whatsoever, . . . (no) theology or scripture or philosophy to balance against the bias of the professor, . . . no experience of real life. (So they) are wholly unfitted to make any judgment on any question of serious import, (and) must think religion and morality out for themselves, through the help of a critical attitude." In short, they needed a Jesuit college education.

This dismissal of all things secular continued through the 1930s, but some analysts did favor softening the Church's policy on education in light of the Great Depression. A "Statement by the Bishops of the Administrative Committees of the National Catholic Welfare Conference on the Present Crisis" (1933) said, among other things, that Catholic schools would just have to do the best they could with their limited resources. They could not emulate "extravagantly conducted tax-paid schools." Yet if they were to counter "chaotic thinking, pagan license, and uncurbed greed," they would need to have more priests on secular campuses making religion "the most attractive of all the subjects taught." Meanwhile, according to a survey conducted at Columbia University and the University of Pennsylvania, Catholic youth were attending non-Catholic institutions primarily because that is where the curricula in which they were interested were available.

Such findings obviously gave the bishops reason to place Catholic chaplains on the secular campus. They had little incentive to do so, however. Those serving as chaplains saw themselves primarily as interim apologists, on hand only until all Catholic students (there were 150,000 on secular campuses in 1940) were being educated on Catholic campuses. Backing this attitude, the unyielding advocates of Catholic institutions continued berating their secular competitors. Then in 1939 Pope Pius XII issued an encyclical entitled *Sertum laetitiae* that supported their demonizing. At the end of World War II, as veterans began matriculating in large numbers, the diatribe intensified. The Jesuits' *America* magazine warned readers how "Lucy's Soul" underwent "an unbalanced progression in knowledge" because a professor with "wide though warped erudition" helped her secular mind to mature but not her religious mind (72: 265-67). Then came rejections of this paranoia. Pax Romana, a Vatican-approved international movement of Catholic students, officially endorsed the Newman Clubs of America; and political theorist John Courtney Murray, S.J., urged them to enhance secular academe with "the ideas that underlie peace and Christian world order" (*America* 75: 28-29).

In other words, post-war American Catholics began to acknowledge that henceforth many of their coreligionists would be attending secular colleges and universities, and that if they continued to dissociate themselves from this larger world it would simply pass them by. At the same time renowned Catholic intellectuals began a counter-movement in favor of greater openness to secular learning. Especially influential was historian John Tracy Ellis's article, "American Catholics and the Intellectual Life" (1955), in which he noted that many Catholic colleges were mediocre. Other scholars offered reasons for this state of affairs, one being the Church's concerted effort to channel its brightest students into the priesthood or religious life, where the celibate lifestyle precluded offspring. Thus did the once dominant separationist ethos gradually lose favor. Its official demise: John Courtney Murray's *We Hold These Truths* (1960). This book offers a powerful defense of American-style separation of religion and state, a doctrine Murray saw validated a few years later in a canon he drafted and the Second Vatican Council endorsed.

These changes in attitude and policy were inspired in part by a multitude of factors over which neither scholars nor ecclesiastical bureaucrats had any control. Among these, the following were crucial: the G.I. Bill that sent veterans flocking into universities; the resulting brick-and-mortar era as campuses expanded exponentially; the baby boom that eventually required even the largest universities to impose limits on their enrollments; the Cold War that inspired the U.S. government to invest profusely in science education, mostly on secular campuses, private and public; and, as a consequence of all of this, the need for even the most traditionally raised young Catholics to prepare for their careers outside the confines of Church-provided learning.

One additional development that is occurring within the confines of American Catholicism is the burgeoning shortfall between the number of lay Catholics and the number of people attracted to the priesthood or to a convent. While the number of Catholics in the US more than doubled from 28 million in 1950 to 59 million in 2000, the total number of priests increased only eight percent (from 43,100 to

46,700) during that time. In the last two decades of the twentieth century a fifth of all priests resigned their ministries, leaving one of every ten parishes without a resident priest. In 1966, nine thousand young men were in the last four years of study for the priesthood; now there are only a third as many. Only 11 percent of the nuns who remain are under forty-five, and more than a quarter of these are over seventy. There are about as many ex-nuns in America as there are nuns, and the unfunded retirement cost of aging religious is approaching $7 billion. The nun-priest ratio, once 5:1, is down to about 2:1; and before long there may be no more nuns at all. (Morris 1997: 292, 301, 310-11, 315-19.)

Taking these data into consideration, one can no longer envision an American Catholic Church maintaining anything like a comprehensive educational program. At the same time, the best secular learning will no longer be found exclusively or even primarily in public schools but rather in various kinds of private schools. Among these will be some supported by the Catholic Church and others supported, for example, by Muslim mosques. In this environment, secularist objections to state funding of sectarian-administered education may become less persuasive than in the past. This is the case in part because of reasons put forward in defense of charter schools. These reasons have been predominantly secular in nature, but they lend themselves to alternative content. In other words, they leave the door ajar for asking: why not put aside concerns about establishment of religion and focus on directing state resources to socially valuable secular curricula regardless of the institutional context in which they are housed? This, in short, is what the charter school movement suggests – and one day soon so might the emerging Muslim schools.

Charter schools are by definition public schools, publicly funded, that are authorized to experiment in their approach to education. Their goal is to be more successful than are the regular public schools. To this end they are exempted from some of the regulations to which the regular schools are subject. First established in the UK in 1988, charter schools began to appear in the US in the early 1990s. They appeared first in Minnesota, then in California; and now some forty US states have charter-school laws. The strongest laws vis-à-vis funding, autonomy, and diversity of charter-granting agencies are in Arizona, California, Colorado, Massachusetts, Michigan, Minnesota, and North Carolina. With few exceptions (namely, Minnesota and New Mexico) funding for charter schools does not achieve parity with regular public ("district") schools.

Charter schools are subject to inconsistent criticisms. They are faulted if they do not perform well enough to justify their draining funds from the public coffer or enjoying a privileged status. If they reduce staff or services to stay within their budgets, though, they are accused of short-changing students (Osberg 2006). The results of empirical assessments, however, have been mixed (e.g., Hill 2006; Brown 2004; NYT 11/23/2004; 'Charter school' in Wikipedia). Among the more vocal opponents are public school teachers. Their stance is understandable as it relates to job maintenance; yet it is somewhat ironic. For, the first US proponent of charter schools, in 1988, was Albert Shanker, president of the American Federation of Teachers. In any event, both proponents and opponents of charter schools have agreed that they must be meticulously secular. Even this, though, is beginning to be rethought.

The secular character of charter schools is neatly spelled out in a New Hampshire statute (Title IX Section 194-B:7) that embodies the US Supreme Court's *Lemon v Kurtzmann* tripartite test. This test, you may remember, defines a constitutional state/religion interaction as one that has a secular purpose, neither advances nor prohibits religion, and exhibits no "excessive entanglement" between school and religion. For the most part charter schools have needed to honor this standard of neutrality to retain their eligibility for public funding. Private schools, by comparison, would presumably be less concerned about this neutrality because they do not depend on public funding. But the process of public funding has itself become highly problematic; and in this context the rules regarding charter schools are beginning to change. In a number of urban areas, Catholic schools facing financial shortfall have been modifying their premises and programs enough to qualify for funds from governments that would otherwise have to provide for an influx of additional students (NYT 3/9/09). Similarly, plans to open charter schools that will teach Hebrew language and culture are underway (NYT 8/24/07; *New Jersey Jewish News*, 3/26/09). Also on the horizon are Muslim charter schools.

Muslim schools that combine a religious orientation with a rigorous secular curriculum are now available in Singapore and will in time spread to other Southeast Asian countries (NYT 4/23/09). And similar schools are being established in the United States. There are not very many Muslim schools in this country, but their numbers are increasing. Exactly how much is somewhat difficult to determine, especially in the wake of 11 September 2001. In the early 1990s estimates as to the Muslim population in the US were in the 5-8 million range (Numan 1992), but are now put at around 2-3 million (Mujahid 2001; Pipes 2001).

The incentive for starting Muslim-based schools is analogous to that of Catholics in the past, namely, to perpetuate religious values that public schools are not able to deal with. For example, even a matter as seemingly minor as a girl wearing a special headgear to school has generated controversial policies which courts inconsistently address (Hamilton 2007: 126-129). So American Muslims, many of whom are middle class, are becoming ever more interested in starting their own private schools, preferably with the financial backing of a voucher system. Indeed, some even contemplate opening sectarian charter schools.

In spite of the constitutional pitfalls to which such a school might be subject (Shelton 2004), a 5-4 US Supreme Court recently endorsed White House funding of faith-based programs in *Hein v Freedom from Religion Foundation* (June 25, 2007). At the same time, however, the US government's use of the Patriot Act to shut down nonprofit organizations that allegedly provide "training" or "material support" to terrorists can be expected to complicate any effort to open and maintain a Muslim-based school (OMB Watch 2003). As this antiterrorism ideology works its way through our society we should be leery of the efforts of the government and other interests as well to control the Internet. For, if successful they will control the process of distance learning that is benefitting so greatly from its present and future capabilities.

What stands out in this attempt to foresee the future configuration of American educational institutions is the likelihood that it will be increasingly complex. This, moreover, will be true not only of the institutions themselves but of their funding mechanisms. It is difficult to imagine how in that complex set of arrangements anyone could implement, say, Robert Audi's secular triad with regard to motivation, rationale, and resolution. Taking the third first, it is indeed imaginable that a school might have an acceptably secular curriculum. As for the second, it is also imaginable that the rationale for setting up such a curriculum would be recognizably secular as well. But by what impartial process would a society go about making sure that the motivation for doing so is sufficiently secular? Even if so stated in all available brochures, might there not be some sectarian motivation lurking in the background (if not the back room) as to the importance of getting our children educated as well as theirs are?

These are, to be sure, just the kinds of questions that hover in the background of any attempt to maintain reasonable state/religion border control. They are, however, ultimately unanswerable because the answers sought could be arrived at only on the basis of suspect determinations as to subjective intent. So rather than pursuing – or, worse, claiming to have obtained – such problematic information, a society should indeed focus on groups as such and on the consequences of their practices on society as a whole.

As we have seen, liberals prefer to associate rights with individuals. For reasons having to do with legal standing, U.S. Supreme Court First Amendment cases typically involve one or more identified individuals. But these cases typically affect particular groups. So it would not be a total departure from this legal history if I were to focus on religious *groups* as the principal agents for bringing the concerns of religion before the state. I don't want to just talk about groups, though. I want to tell you what scholars have written about the rights to which groups as such are entitled. In the final part of this study, then, I will focus on group rights theory and its bearing on state/religion interaction.

PART III
RELIGIOUS GROUPS AND THE PUBLIC SPHERE

Philosophers and judges try hard to set limits on public discourse that affects state-religion relations. So be it. But just what entities are supposed to be bound by these limits? In particular, are these entities individuals or groups? First Amendment cases before the U.S. Supreme Court typically involve one or more individuals in a suit versus an institution. Philosophers usually have individuals in mind when discussing what sort of arguments are properly put before the public. In the world of practical politics as it exists today, however, any individual seeking to communicate with a decision making body is typically a member or a representative of one or more groups that collectively seek to have their preferences made known and, better, translated into policy. And the middle term of their argument is likely to be money or its political equivalent, that is, votes. Moreover, especially over the past several decades in the United States, many groups seeking political objectives are religious. So any view about the morality of religious discourse in the public sphere should take into account the underlying issue of group rights. To this issue, then, I devote the final chapter.

It should be conceded from the outset that some (purportedly) religious groups should if possible be prevented from exercising any influence on government. Since 9/11 there is broad agreement on this point in the United States. But on what principled grounds can one defend such an exclusion knowing that all sorts of questionable interest groups routinely make their preferences known to government and, often enough, get favorable responses not necessarily in the public interest. Is there something so problematic about a religious organization that it requires more assiduous scrutiny?

Liberal theorists in the US, it will be recalled, strongly favor a separationist interpretation of the First Amendment; but they rarely apply this exclusionary preference to state or market interests. Since both government and nongovernment groups of all sorts routinely represent special interests in the public forum, though, exclusion of religious organizations from this decision making process seems undemocratic. For, it arguably violates the free exercise clause with regard to religious groups and perhaps also the nonestablishment clause with respect to secular groups. If such claims have merit, then instead of erecting thicker walls around government decision making one should install more doors and windows. Many worry, however, that this would deprivatize religion and thus risk undermining the secular state.

A totally secular state, as the Soviet Union proved, is undesirable. But as religious nonconformists throughout history could testify, a state-established religion is no more desirable. So to minimize the latter risk, some think privatizing religion is the best way to accommodate diverse worldviews in one and the same society. Liberal theorists, at least, would favor this approach. To achieve it, they envision a decision making apparatus that honors three complementary ideals: an impartial central government (neutrality), the primacy of individuals over nonpublic groups (equality), and selective exclusion of nonpublic groups from the political public sphere (privatization). If implemented, though, these ideals would hinder group advocacy. For, by prioritizing individual liberty, they undercut the political advantage of groups in a participatory democracy and disregard the social importance of political voice. After all, it is the purpose of an interest group to advance the interests of its individual members; and to do this it needs to build bridges between civil society, which is its base, and the governmental sphere. Moreover, religious as well as secular groups engage in such political activism, and arguably they should be free to do so. To make this basic point about participatory democracy I will here draw on group rights theory, and in the process will suggest that the tripartite liberal platform is morally indefensible and politically naive.

Chapter 6
The Political Importance of Interest Groups

An interest group, by definition, is an active pursuer of the interests of its individual members. As such, it presupposes as a given that its members have interests – or needs, or preferences – that differ from those of other citizens in the same society at large. In other words, within society at large different groups of individuals pursue different interests. Such multi-pronged pursuit of interests is not problematic, of course, if meeting everyone's interests is not a zero-sum game, that is, if one group's gain need not require that other groups lose. Where a zero-sum game is being played, however, or at least seems to be, competition among groups becomes problematic. It just so happens, though, that competition among groups of citizens in the same society is quite common. So too are government efforts to keep such competition from disrupting the social order.

At this point, a regulatory mentality might want to sort out the underlying beliefs of each competing group. This, however, is not as easy to accomplish as it sounds. Political parties, special interest groups, unions, and nongovernmental organizations may indeed be motivated by idiosyncratic beliefs as they seek to influence others who believe otherwise. These underlying beliefs may not be articulated, though, as the members of an activist organization go about advocating their preferred policies regarding baby seals or tax cuts, trade agreements or smoking in public. In the event, some underlying beliefs might be better received than others, especially if these involve, say, achieving global dominance or imminent rapture. But arguably this cognitive dissonance is best corrected not by abolishing group input but by enhancing participatory democracy and thereby limiting corporate power.

Populist and/or communitarian support for sociopolitical activity has a long and distinguished history. It originated towards the end of the nineteenth century when social reformers began proposing communal remedies for capitalist-engendered anomie. For example, French sociologist Emile Durkheim defended the importance of what he famously called the division of labor in society (1997; orig.1893). According to Durkheim, the "mechanical" uniformity of primitive societies gives way to "organic" solidarity as different groups focus on different concerns even to the point of separating a realm of the sacred from the profane, as would a religion. In this setting groups with diverse but complementary interests contribute cooperatively to a multifaceted social cohesion.

Drawing on this secular account of religion-like organizations, a number of social scientists began envisioning a polity that includes "intermediate groups" between the state and the individual. After World War II, some American political scientists transformed this view into the pluralist model of interest group democracy. This model would address pluralism by focusing on the functional efficacy of group-assisted government and counting on either competitive or regulatory force to maintain fairness. Pluralism thus managed has been harshly criticized for its elitist conception of democracy and its naive assumptions about how effective such democracy is in practice (e.g., Cawson 1985: 2).

Philosopher Robert Paul Wolff, for example, criticized this "interest-group liberalism" for endorsing institutionalized selfishness rather than "constituting the whole society a genuine group with a group purpose and a conception of the common good." He distinguished two versions of pluralist theory: a "vector-sum" version, which stresses intergroup competition, and a "referee" version, which counts on government to balance competing interests. But he rejected both for being indifferent to the interests of those lacking power (Wolff 1968: 154-61).

To correct such inequitable allocation of political power, public-choice individualists recommend reducing government decision making to a strictly rule-based process. This is why many philosophers who defend liberalism situate only government in the political arena and relegate nonpublic groups to whatever togetherness individuals create in civil society. This arrangement, they say, is as much as nonpublic groups can expect, because they do not belong in the governmental sphere. Thus do liberal accounts of government's role tend to reduce the political public sphere to an abstract meeting place for autonomous individuals whose ability to exercise their rights is somehow guaranteed by government.

This individualist recipe for influencing government seems indifferent to the realities of power distribution. Overlooking the dynamics of public/private interchange, it invites reifying the public as state and disempowering groups other than corporations (see below). People in all walks of life, however, often find that they can achieve some political leverage only in and through groups. Political scientists recognize that these groups are quite active in the affairs of government, but guard the purity of the partition by referring to them as, for example, nongovernment organizations. Such group activism, whatever it is called, would presumably be undermined by an omnicompetent state. But, contrary to Rousseau and his followers, an omnicompetent state is a poor substitute for a government that is receptive and sensitive to constituent demands. It is in this context, then, that one must try to reconcile the diverse goals of interest groups with the need for national unity.

National unity is espoused in various ways, including appeals to holism, egalitarianism, and elitism. Its flaws are corrected by such modifications as representationalism, electoralism, and procedural neutrality. Each of these concepts disparages the role of interest groups, and in so doing helps canonize political exclusivity. The holistic or totalitarian approach reduces society to the state; but micro government is not that easily suppressed. The Nazis, for example, tried to disempower all traditional social organizations; but they established other organizations of their own, the SS being only the most notorious. The result, speaking only of institutional structures, was an administrative chaos in which no one ever knew which agency was responsible for what and policy depended for its consistency and stability on a charismatic leader (Breuilly 1985: 375-377; Sombart 1937: ch. 14).

Avoidance of totalitarianism, then, is a very good reason to favor interest groups. But many social and political philosophers, echoing Rousseau, believe that these bridge institutions create more problems than they solve. For, though two or more groups may cooperate for some purposes, they might also have incompatible interests. At the extreme, such conflict may lead to civil war, something only the weapons and mortuary industries could applaud. But even within the bounds of orderly governance there are good reasons for accommodating dissidence. For, as Alexis de Tocqueville warned, liberty benefits from intermediate institutions between the central state and the individual.

The issue for Tocqueville was straightforward. The revolutionists in France were translating Rousseau's egalitarian demand for plebiscite voting into a Paris-controlled system of government; and this, according to Tocqueville, would inevitably prevent people from solving their problems locally and leave them to the whims of a central bureaucracy. These local institutions had been the instruments through which the landed gentry kept the peasants under their control. But with their abolition decentralization became and has remained a burning issue in France to this day (Tocqueville 1988; Breuilly 1985: 57-61; Zysman 1983: 102-103). It has been presented, for the most part, as involving no significant ethnic diversity. This denial of demographic reality is politically expedient, however, only so long as minorities remain such and can be denied the full rights of citizenship.

Opportunistic xenophobia is not practiced, of course, only in France. It can be observed in many other developed and developing countries, whose boundaries have seldom been based on ethnic homogeneity. In such cases those marginalized may come to believe that achieving their destiny depends on activating their national identity and perfecting it in autonomous statehood. Such reliving of the historically familiar nation-building process on a smaller scale is opposed as anachronistic and impractical by spokespersons of established nation-states as varied as the old Soviet Union and the State of Israel. Each, it so happens, at one time responded to demands for recognition with proposals for less radical restructuring, such as an expanded electorate or a more nuanced confederation. Recently dignified as "liberal nationalism," this ostensibly reasonable posture reveals nonetheless how poorly systematic exclusion prepares those who exercise power to deal with a crisis that political inclusion might have avoided in the first place (Tamir 1993). For this reason alone, if no other, the quest for broader participation in the political process should be encouraged.

Towards this end, Hannah Arendt reluctantly endorsed representative governm[ent]. Characterizing unilaterally government-originated policy as violence, she insisted legitimate political power must be based on "an opinion upon which many publicly ar[e in] agreement." Political power on this view is not a momentary or transitory phenomenon, s[uch] as a biennial vote, but requires ongoing citizen activism. It can prosper only "where words [are] not used to violate and destroy but to establish relations and create new realities. Power [so] understood] is what keeps the public realm . . . in existence". Persuaded, however, [that] populism is not in the public interest if the people are ill prepared, Arendt settled [on] representative government as a reasonable alternative provided the representatives can t[hink] beyond their own interests. This precludes viewing an elite as just another interest group. [But] it allows for an elite that consists, for example, of eugenicist rulers who claim to represe[nt a] "master race" (Arendt 1963: 234-51; 1958: 197-207).

Under more typical capitalist-dominated arrangements, the operative agenda of a ru[ling] elite is not so easily specified. Is it, for example, unified or, what is more likely, intern[ally] divided? Does it operate within or outside of government, or both? Is it merely advisor[y or] actually determinative of policy to be applied to everyone? Think tanks are suggestive in [this] regard: though structurally on the periphery, they may in practice be very influential appenda[ges] of government. Given the opacity of such peripheral influence, Arendt's proposed mode[l of] communicative decision-making cannot easily be applied to the complex interrelationships [that] characterize modern political activity. For, says Jürgen Habermas, instead of accommoda[ting] this complexity, she envisioned "rigid conceptual dichotomies between 'public' and 'priv[ate,'] state and economy, liberty and welfare, political-practical activity and production" (1983: 1[ ]). One pole of such dichotomies is said to be an area of "private" decision-making free f[rom] government interference. A claim to privacy is made, however, in a social context of wh[ich] government is a part. To circumscribe government in this context, it has been customar[y] identify an area -- often called civil society -- into which government should not ordinarily intrude but which is itself taken into account in the constitutional order of things. Karl Marx knew this convention well; but he tended to equate civil society with the working class, which he counted on to generate a revolution.

A rulers/workers dichotomy is, of course, an oversimplification, as Friedrich Engels already acknowledged. And as various neo-Marxist scholars concede, government itself might exercise some power. Alternatively, liberals counter the Marxist dichotomy by insisting that the elite is not a ruling class because it is open to competent persons from any level of society. On this view, family origins do not predetermine career opportunities: incompetent children of rulers fall by the wayside; competent children of the ruled rise to positions of power. This truism exaggerates the opportunities for inclusion in the ruling group, however, and in no way modifies the latter's status as ruler, clearly distinguishable as a group from the ruled. Some theorists, though, especially those associated with political pluralism, have argued that politically active intermediate groups can counteract the sense of powerlessness so prevalent in modern societies.

The activist American philosopher John Dewey, for example, rejected "individualistic liberalism" as an inadequate response to socioeconomic elitism and called for institutions that could influence without becoming subordinated to the political process. Following Dewey in this respect, economist John Kenneth Galbraith (1963) thought major corporations had become such dominant forces in society that a strong regulatory government could be avoided only if such intermediate institutions as labor unions could function as a "countervailing power" in the private sphere. This was essentially the position that Durkheim (1959: ch 8; 1957) arrived at after having long defended centralization as the process whereby law evolves into organic solidarity. Each of these views assumes that an effective intermediary group, though rooted in the private sphere, must somehow be operationally public.

This assumption has merit in that the unaffiliated individual is ordinarily politically impotent whereas individuals who are affiliated with an activist organization can exercise political influence indirectly. Too often, unfortunately, that organization's influence may be based largely on its superior weaponry. In more civilized societies, though, the ability to fund political campaigns is likely to be a more important factor. For over a century in the Unit States – roughly, from 1828 to 1971 – exceptionally wealthy individuals ("Fat Cats," in t political jargon) were the principal source of campaign funds and so recipients of politic favors. Reforms during that period tended for the most part to undermine the efforts of othe notably, union leaders, to become a countervailing force.

A meaningful albeit limited step towards legitimate reform was effected by The Fede Election Campaign Act of 1971 – amended in 1976 and again by the Bipartisan Campai Reform Act of 1979. This legislation sought to impose limits on donors, transacti arrangements, and transparency of money for electioneering. Finding that money is spee (protected under the First Amendment), the U.S. Supreme Court rejected having a ceiling eith on the overall amount raised or on the amount the candidate personally contributes (*Buckley Valeo*, 424 U.S. 1, 1976). Other constraints on funding arrangements are in place, though; a this has led to the flowering of political action committees (PACs). These PACs are t intermediary instruments through which today's more anonymous Fat Cats, especially the t management of major corporations, exercise as a group even more political control than d their highly visible forebears in times past.

It is a given in this respect that big business is becoming ever more politically astute, control of social arrangements ever more complete. This is especially so now that most workin people are directly or indirectly dependent on large corporations for their livelihood. What regrettable, then, is not that labor has organized but that its organizing has been so limite especially in the United States (Byrne 1990). Moreover, businesses and unions are not the on organizations that articulate and defend the interests of a set of constituents whose speci problems might not otherwise be addressed. Given this de facto political configuratio individuals who want their interests represented effectively need to enter the public sphere a group. Assuming that all who wish to do this can do so, however, might not the resulti group-based dialogue engender more problems than it solves?

Politically active groups, some fear, might come to exercise too much control ov public policy. For, a government's component agencies are susceptible to "capture" organizations that want their private interests converted into public policy. This would n happen, though, if such organizations were effectively monitored and held accountable, if need be by the state. For example, after a long history of official hostility to unions, the U.S. federal government finally recognized and for a time supported the right to organize as a useful instrument for maintaining industrial peace, in part because it monitors union activity. Also (purportedly) monitored are almost all groups, including PACs, that seek to influence public policy to the advantage of those whom they represent. Besides, even apart from formal regulatory constraints, a group accustomed to influencing public policy, such as the National Rifle Association (NRA), is unlikely to remain indifferent to well organized opposing views. Indeed, no group however public-spirited its cause can escape opposition from others whose interests they threaten. So the mere fact that a nongovernmental group has political influence is not a sufficient reason to question its right to participate in a meaningful way in decision-making processes that affect those whom it represents.

This said, if a group seeks to advance the public good via political communication, it should be held publicly accountable. Achieving public accountability depends, in turn, on a mix of structural and procedural arrangements that assures open communication. These can vary depending on whether an interest group is local or functional or both. Concentration on a particular geographical locale may enable people to control the resources they need for their mutual well-being without relying on either laissez-faire "private" property or state-managed "public" ownership (Anton et al. 2000). But "strong democracy" (Barber 1984) requires establishing ways to resolve conflicts between functional and local assessments of a problem and between diverse interests that happen to be in close geographical proximity. In particular, establishing proportional representation for electoral purposes would reflect diverse interests rather than geography, thereby giving voice to women and minorities more effectively than can be done in a district-based system. A functional group, finally, can sometimes make a special contribution even to the solution of a local problem by virtue of its familiarity with similar problems in other locales.

Nonpublic groups should be encouraged, then, to participate in the political process. Their participation should be circumscribed, though, to prevent it from undermining impartiality in government. Towards this end, first, a clear distinction should be made between a group's claiming special benefits and its claiming equal access and voice as a group. Claims to special benefits have been falling out of favor, especially as a basis for remedying past discrimination (see *Parents Involved in Community Schools Inc. v. Seattle School District and Meredith v. Jefferson County, KY*, 2007, 551 U.S. ___). Group access and voice is still salient, though, e.g., in connection with thresholds for a political party's inclusion on a ballot and for religion/state interaction. The underlying issues raised by a claim to access and voice are illuminated by Owen Fiss's argument for judicial recognition of groups and Will Kymlicka's argument for their being politically recognized in a liberal society.

Fiss (1976) assumed that our government should redress extreme maldistribution of wealth and that the U.S. Constitution can be interpreted in support of its doing so. From this currently disparaged perspective, he looked for ways in which the U.S. Supreme Court might facilitate maintaining equal protection of the laws. This led him to propose a "group-disadvantaging principle": the collective needs of a long disadvantaged group should be taken into account in deciding if state action that has a "differential impact" on members of that group is constitutional. Judges prefer an individualistic interpretation, he claims, because it is easy to apply and as such is purportedly more rational, objective, and value neutral. But, he contends, by systematically denying the reality of groups in society, this approach fails to address some of the most oppressive institutional forms of racial discrimination, notably any blanket exclusion of a group from socially significant facilities that are government-supported.

An approach attentive to groups, Fiss argues, can better deal with the economic and political subordination of a racial minority. But would it not invite a potentially unlimited number of groups to contest their subordinate status? No, he thinks, because even though the Fourteenth Amendment applies explicitly not just to blacks but to any "person", the Court could limit standing to groups whose members are interdependent as well as being disfavored under the law. In particular, he would limit standing to subordinate "natural" groups (among which he would include women) as distinguished from "artificial" groups that are actually created by law (for instance, people who happen to be in a particular income-tax bracket) (Fiss 1976: 173).

Constitutional theory aside, restricting the remedial agenda to "natural" groups is problematic. Scientists no longer agree on any empirical basis for racial differences (Blum 2002, ch. 7). Similarly, the once commonsense assertion of a sexual dichotomy without nuance is now subject to intense debate among feminists (e.g., Butler 1990; Nussbaum 1999) and gay rights advocates (e.g., Phelan 1989). So whether a disadvantaged group is considered "natural" or "artificial," its very identity is largely a matter of cultural recognition. For, what is at issue is the politics of classification: who does the classifying and for what goals or purposes. In constitutional terms, First Amendment free speech rights do not automatically translate into Fifth or Fourteenth Amendment due process rights. But suppression of the one may amount to the other, as, for example, if government chose not to take the concerns of HIV/AIDS or Agent Orange victims seriously. To decree that some politically defended classification merits no political standing is to limit the interests that can be effectively represented in a society.

This, some believe, may be only a temporary obstacle to justice, since it is now possible for a virtually unlimited number of individuals to communicate with one another and with their government through technological links. And indeed the political influence of web-based organizations is now beyond dispute. But giving a technology-based voice to the otherwise disempowered individual is not enough. A credible public sphere must accommodate groups, not merely as polled individuals but as designated agents through which individuals participate collectively in meaningful political discourse.

This collective involvement is a key feature of Will Kymlicka's defense of the rights of minority groups, including in particular indigenous and francophone peoples in Canada. Rejecting post-World War II interpretations of liberalism as both too individualistic and too statist in orientation, Kymlicka uses liberal support for equal rights and resources in a nation-state "to defend minority rights in multinational states" (Kymlicka 1989a: 2-5, 127, 169). For, in most supposedly "unified" states the citizens belong to readily distinguishable cultural groups, indifference to which in the name of equal rights of citizenship may be nothing more than a mask for dominance. The stronger the effort to "integrate" these groups, the harder they struggle for autonomy. Consider, for example, Muslims, Croats and Serbs in the former

Yugoslavia, Basques in Spain, Irish Catholics in Protestant-dominated Ulster, Sephardic Jews and Palestinians in Israel (Tamir 1993).

In short, Kymlicka defines a nation in cultural and ethnic terms, and endorses culture as contextual support for individuals' liberty. A cultural community constitutes a primary good, provided it enhances "meaningful individual choice." This modest plea for "differential citizenship rights" seems to tilt the traditional liberal concept of "equality before the law." But, he argues, official acknowledgement of a group need only recognize unequal circumstances (such as those of indigenous as compared to immigrant citizens in Canada). This recognition merely accentuates what liberals themselves acknowledge at least implicitly: "that the free individual is only possible within a culture of freedom" (Kymlicka 1989: 75, 143-45, 169-72, 207, 227).

A group, finally, may hope to achieve something like sovereignty. But scholars are divided as to whether any such political objective merits support. Communitarians tend to favor group rights as an alternative to centralized government, so might well envision a United States of America organized as "a federation of groups rather than a community of citizens" (Walzer 1983: 150). Centrist liberals would object to any such group-differentiated polity, in part, to preclude the disproportionate advantage those organized into groups would have over those not organized or at least not as well. Such concern about disproportionate advantage merits attention; but, for the record, it does not justify denying political voice to a group merely because it is religious in orientation. For, this concern might well inspire a differently oriented group to become involved in the public decision making process. This outcome is especially desirable if the newer participant pursues objectives that are recognizably for the public good.

In short, liberal political theorists worry that allowing interest groups a political role negatively impacts both personal fulfillment and national unity. Even if such is the case, societies are becoming ever more complex as diverse groups strive to be taken seriously and structure themselves to this end. So liberals need to accommodate such political diversity at least enough to recognize a role for nongovernment groups in forming and carrying out public policy. Any given group may indeed threaten the ideal of a well ordered society. But taken collectively groups may constitute an enriched approach to equality by attending to particular concerns not adequately addressed by official policy. So whether a group has a right to exist and act politically, even if it is religiously based, is a legitimate moral question.

Chapter 7

The Moral Need for Groups in a Modern Democracy

Liberals tend not to have a place for activist religious groups in their political universe – nor, in fact, for any other group as such. For, as noted, they ordinarily adopt an individualist perspective when discussing democracy. Some say, for example, that talk about the rights and obligations of a group is meaningful only if reinterpreted to mean those of individual members of the group. To them, a group is a legal fiction used to protect individuals associated with it from liabilities to which they would otherwise be subject. Some social philosophers do acknowledge, though, that groups are not just the aggregate of their individual members (e.g., Held 1984; May 1987; Feinberg 1990; Ingram 2000). Implicit in these disagreements are issues regarding individual moral responsibility for a group's action or inaction. In terms of negative duties ("thou shalt not"), such responsibility underlies the felony murder rule: if a killing occurs during the perpetration of a non-homicidal felony, each participant may be charged with murder. There are limits, though, on an individual's responsibility for collective behavior, as can be illustrated by relating liberal doctrines about affirmative duties ("thou shalt") to the murder of Kitty Genovese.

Thirty-eight residents of Kew Gardens (Queens, New York; 1964) heard their co-resident screaming while she was being sequentially stabbed to death just outside their apartment building. None came to her aid, nor did anyone telephone the police. Some said they did not want to "get involved"; and no doubt all feared for their own lives. Third party assessments have been censorious (NYT 3/27/1964; Rosenthal 1999). But liberal theory offers no reliable grounds for recrimination. Ms. Genovese's assailant certainly violated her rights, but those who heard her screams would not ordinarily be expected to do anything likely to be ineffectual and/or harmful to them.

Being private citizens, say individual-oriented ethicists, they were free to mind their own business and were not obliged to become involved with local law enforcement.

Kantian ethicists do assign each individual a generic ("imperfect") duty to help others in some way. But one's choice of beneficiaries need not be crime victims or, this category having been selected, Kitty Genovese in particular. Even if the Kew Gardens residents had formed a Neighborhood Crime Watch, each person's decision to participate would presumably have been voluntary; and, except for the participant "on duty," no one else's failure to intervene would necessarily be morally blameworthy. But would this exoneration apply to the only able-bodied person in the vicinity? And if not, how large must a group be to justify exonerating a negligent individual (cf. Fishkin 1982 ch. 10; French 1991:145-85, 251-86)? If we take human frailty into account in addressing such matters we would at least avoid adopting a rigid rule of law; and, inversely, we would hopefully be sympathetic towards a group whose members share responsibility for defending one another's lives, especially if they strive to do so only by means of actions that are arguably also for the broader public good. But we would surely hesitate to condone the self-contained ethos of a clan or gang without subjecting it to modifications based on human rights. In other words, it is no easy task to interconnect an individual's moral responsibility and that of his or her group; but some scholars do try.

Larry May, among others, has argued that an individual member of a group may be responsible at least indirectly for actions or omissions for which other members of the group are directly responsible, thereby constituting a kind of social responsibility. In particular, he argues that anyone who helps create a "climate of opinion" that endorses hostility towards someone, e.g., because of his or her race, is at least partially responsible for any harm that is directly traceable to this collective mind set. What Kitty Genovese needed, however, was not just a favorable climate of opinion in her regard but effective intervention. Task-oriented professionals, e.g., security guards, have a prima facie obligation to provide such intervention; but what if none is nearby? Is not a nearby non-professional obligated to bring a problem of which he or she is aware to the attention of relevant professionals (Feinberg 1991)? Perhaps so in principle, but this assumes that one is living in a well-ordered, equitable society in which none is marginalized and officialdom routinely responds to people's needs. What if one does not live in such a society – or neighborhood? What then?

Had the Kew Gardens group been an extended family, or a moiety or clan, or members of a close-knit religious sect, they might well have responded -- directly rather than by phoning agents of the police power that most liberals say must reside exclusively with the state. Whether the neighborhood in question had any reason to count on expeditious police intervention is also relevant; for if the neighborhood is in what amounts to a Hobbesian state of nature, then appropriate self-defense becomes an acceptable if not mandatory alternative to unfulfilled promises of crime control.

John Stuart Mill might even have endorsed such group-based self-help as a proper application of the duty of benevolence he found to be among our fundamental social values. Egalitarians would become uneasy, however, if an on-site Kitty Genovese Memorial Neighborhood Watch sought official endorsement of its activities. For, these activities involve a nonpublic group exercising quasi-public power and thereby possibly putting society as a whole at risk, as do uncontrolled militias.

Such decentralization of the police power raises questions about the appropriate scope of a sub-national group's prerogatives and/or about the wisdom of making sovereignty the sole determinant of power, which has troubled political theorists – and gun rights proponents – for centuries (Stapleton, 1995). Tangential to these concerns is another as to the ethical propriety of dealing directly with any sub-national group – be it a labor union, a corporation, a clan, or whatever – so long as other individuals not members of that group have no comparable representation. This, after all, is a common if not typical situation; and it is fraught with ethical ramifications that need to be examined before attempting to circumscribe the political role of religious groups.

First a preliminary observation: where groups represent the interests of their members before government, the exclusion of non-members from access and voice is prima facie discriminatory. Such non-members may be discriminated against, however, not deliberately and for cause but only because of flaws in the process of group representation. These flaws are problematic insofar as they are allowed to exist even though they distribute power unequally among interest groups and unaffiliated individuals; and as such they should be modified to expand people's political access and voice.

In this regard there are at least six difficulties to which an egalitarian can point: (1) procedures that are fair on paper may not be so as practiced; (2) if only some interests are represented organizationally, those not so represented will be even more disempowered; (3) so long as resources are unequally distributed, some groups are likely to dominate over and even neutralize the input of others; (4) some people are so lacking in resources necessary to achieve organizational representation that their marginalization would increase in direct proportion to others' ability to organize; (5) even if an interest is represented organizationally, the organization may itself be internally undemocratic in its own decision-making processes; and (6) if all possible interests were in fact organized and given access to the public decision making process, the process would grind to a halt.

The first difficulty relates to background conditions for interest group politics. It is all too true: **procedures that are fair on paper might be otherwise in practice**. Some might write this off by saying that it is impossible in principle to accommodate everyone's preferences. Still political theorists continue looking for ways to practice majority rule without unduly excluding anyone from the policy making process (Buchanan and Tullock 1965). These quests for fairness may be undermined, however, by expert manipulation of whatever set of rules are in effect or, more fundamentally, by skewing basic procedures..

As an example of rule manipulation, in the early 1970s Indiana enacted a law allowing state employees to bargain collectively; but the state Supreme Court invalidated the new law on the grounds that one provision was unconstitutional and (conveniently) the final version of the bill lacked a severability clause that would have allowed the remaining provisions to stand. (To this day no statutory law has been enacted, although from 1989 till 2005 gubernatorial executive orders authorized collective bargaining.)

On the federal level, in the late 1980s the U.S. Congress raised procedural unfairness to a new level. Having increased social security taxes to prepare the fund for baby-boomers who will retire in the second decade of the twenty-first century, members of Congress began to worry that the huge surplus thus created would be a tempting target in the interim. So they adopted a set of protective measures: the fund was taken "off budget" and a "super-majority" (60 votes in the Senate) was required for any legislation involving that fund. But two words ("as reported") inserted into this legislation make it applicable only to a budget bill as reported out of committee and not to any such bill as amended on the floor.

A final case in point is the legislatively created conflict between the Privacy Act of 1974 and the Freedom of Information Act of 1966 (amended 1974, 1976). Under the FOIA an agency need not release otherwise covered information if it does not technically "possess" that information; but, inversely, it has the discretion to release information that falls under any of nine categories of privacy-protecting exemptions (Hixson 1987: 184, 191-92).

Such manipulations of procedure obviously undermine efforts to maintain a fairness standard for group access to government. But these manipulations are trivial compared to the deliberate constraints on democracy built into the US Constitution. For, this hallowed document contains provisions that render grossly unfair several of our principal government institutions, including the US presidency (an office filled by an inherently undemocratic Electoral College) and the US Senate (made up of members most of whom represent states where comparatively few citizens reside). Whether these institutions can be reformed in less than a millennium is debatable. Other denials of fairness may, however, be more amenable to correction. One of these would be to undo the post-World War II legislation that in the guise of assuring workers a "bill of rights" has greatly disempowered labor unions; and facilitating religious groups' political activity would require rethinking various interpretations of constitutional constraints. Meanwhile, few comparable constraints have been imposed on major corporations even though they are themselves or they control the most politically influential interest groups.

If indeed the principal beneficiary of this procedural shell game is our corporate oligarchy, the principal victim is substantive democracy. There are remedies for this, but they involve much more than a liberal dose of procedural fairness. Desirable as this may be, it obviously cannot serve as a basis for participatory democracy unless it is carried out in an institutional context that protects disadvantaged interests against forces that can ignore what they have to say with impunity. For, a disadvantage might not involve any inherent inadequacy, e.g., as to reasoning ability, but only insufficient resources (the fourth difficulty, considered below).

The second difficulty is that any political configuration in which some but not all interests are represented does tend to disempower those excluded. Other things being equal, **members of an organized group have a distinct advantage over people who are not organized**. And the more effectively interest groups influence public policy, the more completely are the interests of unaffiliated individuals disregarded by default. This, however, is not an insurmountable obstacle to procedural fairness.

Some corrective guidance may be found in proposals to rationalize procedures, and perhaps even more in the simple fact that government is never definitively sealed off from "outsider" input. In other words, the practical solution involves maximizing equitable interest input, and this requires revising norms for communicating that are unnecessarily discriminatory. At issue here are hurdles that the less astute have difficulty surmounting, e.g., regarding which form to fill out, in which bureau to file a complaint, which statute to use as the basis of a claim, and so on. Removing such encrustations of bureaucracy would, presumably, benefit unaffiliated individuals quite apart from their religious preferences.

The third difficulty noted about interest group politics is also manifestly true: **some organized groups achieve better results for themselves than do other organized groups.** The underlying problem is this: the mere existence of an interest group is no guarantee of its enjoying equal representation; groups, like individuals, are differently accommodated. For example, during the 1990-91 U.S. Senate Ethics Committee hearings regarding the so-called Keating Five, it became clear that not all constituents of a public official have equal access to or persuasive power over that official. And it became clearer a decade later when Vice-President Cheney, in time supported by court decisions, claimed executive privilege as a reason for not releasing any information about energy policy meetings he held primarily with oil industry executives. As these instances illustrate, transparency is hardly a common characteristic of governmental process. And this is a serious hindrance to democratic decision-making, in part because it is sometimes difficult to determine whether a decision making body is governmental or is otherwise subject to governmental constraints.

The difficulty in question can be illustrated by a series of court decisions regarding the Boy Scouts of America (BSA), which on a national level receives about a fourth of its funding from the Catholic Church and not coincidentally discriminates against gays, agnostics, and atheists. In 1998 the California Supreme Court ruled unanimously that the Mount Diablo Council of BSA is not a business so is free to discriminate against homosexuals and atheists. And in 2000 the U.S. Supreme Court ruled that New Jersey had no right to interfere with the BSA's discriminatory policies (530 U.S. 640). But in 2006 the California Supreme Court ruled unanimously that because the city of Berkeley was providing the BSA sea scouts a free berth at its marina it could bar the BSA's discriminatory policies. Some religious conservatives find such constraints unduly biased and oppressive; but before they throw their baby out with the bath water they should reflect most carefully on the widespread practice in the Bush administration (2001-2009) of appointing individuals to decision making positions in government on the basis not of their competence but of their commitment to conservative religious preferences.

These line-crossing issues show how important it is to establish ethically structured institutions in and through which citizens can participate in the formulation and implementation of public policy. These existed during the Middle Ages in the form of guilds, churches, and estates; but liberal governments disempowered all of these by abolishing them, or extending their once special privileges to all, or transferring their power to the state. In the twentieth century, however, many agencies were established that are not neatly public or private by liberal criteria yet they exercise essentially governmental functions without accountability to the people. For this reason, they should be monitored in what Jürgen Habermas calls "the public sphere of the entire public," because cumulatively they transform societal power into political power. (Breuilly 1985: 356, 377-79; Habermas 1989.)

Some interests, having achieved legitimacy in large established institutions, are well entrenched in the legitimation lore of democratic societies. Somewhat less secure are charitable foundations and labor unions. Unions in particular used to be the establishment's favorite example of egalitarian democracy gone awry; but protected minorities have become a preferred target of acrimony. For half a century the latter were indeed benefitting from the courts' endorsement of affirmative action. But from the outset social conservatives opposed to this concept an abstract egalitarianism that favors no group whatsoever; and this position is now that of the U.S. Supreme Court. This imaginary egalitarianism is, however, selective: rights readily accorded to some groups are commonly deemed inappropriate for others.

A comparison between the U.S. Supreme Court's accommodation of the politically abstemious Amish communities and its hostility towards Japanese-Americans during World War II, then towards American Communist Party members during the Cold War era is illustrative in this regard. But so is the Court's ruling that only individuals claiming harm, and not groups, can sue to force compliance with environmental laws (Stone 1974). Then, finally, there are government employees, whom legislators and courts have long kept politically disempowered.

Originally passed in 1939 as the Hatch Act to protect government employees against political coercion by their superiors, this law (and the state-level copies of it known as Little Hatch Acts) has effectively prevented federal and federally paid state employees from participating (other than by voting) in electoral politics. Such depoliticizing of the government bureaucracy helps preserve its image as impartial servant of the people; but it does not prevent its being used for political purposes. And considering the education- and interest-level of government employees, it also neutralizes a source of informed opposition. So it is commendable that courts have begun to relax these rigid constraints somewhat.

In defense of selective egalitarianism, one might argue that not all interests are equally important, especially in times of crisis. This opens the door, however, to callous disregard of differences and, in the extreme case, to a small subset of groups dominating over all others. If raw political power is the deciding factor, this can of course happen, either with regard to a single issue or with regard to all issues decided in the public forum. Fortunately, no one group is likely to dominate all others indefinitely, as even the NRA has come to realize in its longstanding opposition to gun control legislation. But the hegemony of one special interest is by no means impossible, especially if it has access to means of coercion. Such undemocratic possibilities intensify the need for other interest groups, be they religious or secular in orientation.

It is also possible, finally, for groups to improve their effectiveness through various membership strategies. According to economist Mancur Olson (1971) the size of a group is inversely proportional to its effectiveness. He attributed this size-related inefficiency to what would now be called a free rider problem, and argued that this problem can be overcome by offering members special benefits, as do labor unions and industry-specific organizations. Whether he would extend this reasoning to groups that stress other-worldly benefits is difficult to say. In anticipation of the next difficulty, however, he would expect groups to pay their own way and not look to government to remedy shortfalls in their budgets (Olson 1982).

The fourth difficulty survives this appeal to self-help because **an imbalance in interest representation is often traceable to an unequal distribution of resources.** Otherwise unrepresented individuals can diminish their exclusion, though, in a number of ways. They can, for example, pool their limited resources by paying dues to an appropriate advocacy organization, including one that uses the Internet skillfully to convey the preferences of its members at a comparatively small cost. Analogously, any group that by its very nature has comparatively few members – one, say, that concerns itself with victims of a rare disease -- can enter into coalitions with others similarly situated -- in the case indicated, by joining with other rare disease groups (to win support, for example, for government underwriting of so-called orphan drug manufacture). Such organizations are sometimes given some government subsidies, such as the awarding of attorneys' fees in successful, if not in all, non-trivial lawsuits brought in the interest of its constituents (May 1987: 169-78). The inability of some people to achieve representation of their interests is due, however, not to lack of numbers but to a devastating lack of resources that not even their numbers can surmount, as was once the lot of the majority in South Africa and is now so in Zimbabwe.

In such instances, justice may require that those unable to organize be provided public funds in order to organize in their own behalf. To this end, Iris Marion Young recommended an affirmative action program for oppressed groups. What is needed, she contends, is a "heterogeneous public," through which certain otherwise powerless social groups would be publicly recognized, funded, and included in deliberations regarding matters that affect the lives of their members. A truly social group in her terms is based on shared practices or a way of life rather than on the contractual affiliation of a belief-based "ideological" group or a project-oriented interest group. The distinctions are not clear cut, however, and groups of different types might overlap or even succeed one another. What is crucial for Young, however, is that government should assist only groups whose constituents are oppressed, the others, presumably, being able to tend to their interests without public assistance (Young 1990 and 1986).

Young's proposal would in effect favor one group over others and thus be vulnerable to a charge of "reverse discrimination" because it unfairly penalizes those who are not members of that group. More broadly, her reliance on public funding invites opponents to raise all the usual objections directed against the welfare state. But, as noted, introducing yet another organized interest into the political process tips the balance unfairly against others only if the others have an indisputable claim on all their advantages.

The fifth difficulty involves assessing the propriety of screening out of interest group politics those **groups that are not themselves democratically organized**. This is a very serious problem, and it is often though by no means uniquely associated with religious groups. But somewhat as the European Union deals with countries seeking membership, one might offer such a group political access and voice once it has corrected unacceptable flaws in its accommodation of individual members. Thus, for example, some proponents of group rights would deny such rights to a group that does not treat its members fairly and humanely and does not allow them to leave the group freely (Ingram 2000: 89). Some groups, it so happens, would not easily satisfy such a proviso, e.g., an ethnic group culturally committed to female genital mutilation or the group (DEAF) that fosters perpetuation of the American Sign Language (ALS) and to that end opposes educational mainstreaming of the children of deaf parents (Ingram 2000, 71-78). Of course, those opposed to group rights point to such situations to show why an individual's interests ought on principle trump those of a group whenever the two conflict. In this regard, many religious groups (as also the erstwhile Soviet Union) severely restrict their members' choice to stay or leave; so I will return to this issue below.

The sixth difficulty with regard to group-based politics is on its face procedural in nature in that it seeks to avoid **uncontrolled multiplication of groups**

that might make group-government interaction impossible. This concern would be surmounted, presumably, if a society had a priori criteria for determining which groups are entitled to participate in the political process. In reality, though, a new group typically emerges in response to a shared frustration experienced by individuals with common interests. So if left-handed redheads have concerns that others do not recognize, an interest group committed to articulating those concerns could emerge. If it did, government would not need to determine prima facie the merits of these concerns but the significance of its constituents' raising them. Thus in the early 1990s emerging interest groups in the UK kept unwanted roads from being built and more recently Alaskan natives have united in opposition to an oil drilling proposal that threatens their way of life.

In brief, interest groups are vital components of a democratic decision-making process. Realistically, they don't all have equal influence. But their right to a hearing should not depend on their respective monetary contributions. Nor should they be distinguished in terms of their being public or nonpublic. All interest groups are public insofar as they seek to affect public policy. Allowing for appropriate standards of accountability, the individual privacy of a group's members should be respected so long as the group causes no substantive harm to society at large. And merely advocating a particular policy, however disconcerting to others, is not harmful in this way. Moreover, a pluralist society can't arrive at and act on policy that is legitimately for the public good without accommodating diversity. But as I have noted at length, not everyone who welcomes pluralist influences on public policy would extend this open stance to religious groups. What remains to consider, then, is whether and how they too can be accommodated.

Chapter 8
Religious Groups in the Political Process

Should religious groups be free to advocate their preferences in political circles? In actual practice, they do so in many polities; but around the world some are tolerated even as others are oppressed. For example, Shi'ite Muslims are politically dominant in Saudi Arabia and in Iran; but neither country is very tolerant of other religious groups. In China, the government sponsors an official church (called the Three-Self Patriotic Movement); and it also tries very hard to keep independently started "house churches" from achieving any real influence, e.g., by limiting their meetings to a maximum of twenty-five persons and denying them the right to own property (*Washington Post*, 1 Oct. 2006). By contrast, The Netherlands has established a "pillarization" system that favors (only) three distinct groups organized to effect people's well-being in society: protestant, catholic, and humanist (Rémond 1999: 192). In the United States, though separation of state and religion is mandatory, religious groups nonetheless influence many government policy decisions.

In short, religious groups are diversely accommodated in different public arenas. Meanwhile, theorists debate whether and how religious groups should be tolerated. In the United States, at least, they worry about balancing equality and merit even as some insist that toleration of diversity should be inclusive. This, however, is easier asserted than justified in the West. For, the very presence of a religious group in the public arena runs counter to centuries of history the net effect of which was first to accommodate and then, in the wake of extreme abuses, to prohibit such political access. And that is why certain religious groups, including in particular the Church of England, were at the forefront of efforts in the twentieth century to legitimate group rights above and beyond mere tolerance (Figgis 1997; Stapleton 1995).

Toleration, or tolerance, may be defined as a deliberate non-exercise of power against others of whom one disapproves and whose ability to thrive or even to exist would otherwise be compromised. These others may be disapproved because of some observable difference from those exercising power (e.g., their race or sex) or because they have different beliefs or practices. Regarding observable differences, toleration may be equated with a positive obligation to help those who are disadvantaged to thrive (Scarman 1987). It is more commonly focused on atypical beliefs or practices, be they religious or political.

Religious tolerance in particular achieved the status of a social value only after centuries of sectarian bloodletting gave way in modern times to a fairly rigid separation of religion and state. This separation, as we have seen, became standard policy in the West only after centuries of arrangements whereby governments used a favored religion for political purposes. This arrangement first existed in the form of gods that people invented and paid homage to as far back as prehistoric times. In the more immediate past, Roman Emperor Constantine and Eastern tetrarch Licinius issued the Edict of Milan (313 CE) to replace government-sanctioned religious persecution with what became acceptance of Christianity.

De facto this endorsement applied only to proper Christians. So it did shift the political polarity of Christianity from negative to positive in the Roman Empire but also led to centuries of Christian intolerance of deviant beliefs (Lecky 1955). Medieval imperialists used a doctrine of two swords (church and state) to maintain politically desirable thought control. Then during the Reformation the Augsburg Interim of 1555 regionalized that doctrine by authorizing each local ruler to determine and preserve religious orthodoxy (*cujus regio, ejus religio*). Not only non-Christians but even Christians with regionally disfavored beliefs were brutally executed by the thousands for government defined crimes of heresy (more despicable to Catholics) or blasphemy (more offensive to Protestants). At the turbulent onset of disaffiliation and reformism, sectarian pogroms identified entire groups as their target. In time, the proliferation of sects made collective identification of the enemy increasingly hazardous even to ruling cliques. So individuals came to be recognized as more expedient targets of intolerance, with the help of a theoretical distinction between thought and action now commonplace in judicial determinations of the scope of free speech (Levy 1993). Collective intolerance is, however, by no means extirpated from human experience, as can be seen in such tribalizations of religion as formerly in Northern Ireland (Fitt 1987) and today in Iraq.

As such situations make clear, doctrinaire suppression is still enough of a threat to support liberal distrust of even secular intermediate groups that might advise government how to define the terms and conditions of orthodoxy. Thus traditional liberals are altogether comfortable with pluralism only if its sectarian components are privatized. But privatization is a two-edged sword. For, it insulates government not only from sectarian conflict but from the influence of any and all groups with religious sensitivities. In other words, it restricts influence over government decision-making to secularists.

To prevent such secularist suppression of diversity, some recommend representative democracy; but in practice this arrangement is not easily distinguishable from elitism. This is especially the case if a parliamentary system disintegrates into a ritualistic endorsement of administrative fiat. For example, if the mainstream British view were to prevail, all government decision-making would be securely locked inside a "public sector" into which no private interests could slip if not invited. Rejecting this "democratic centralism," one opposition MP noted: "If all power is concentrated in the hands of the state and its agencies, and those agencies are in turn controlled by the Party -- even a supposedly socialist Party -- we have the very antithesis of socialism, the denial of power to the ordinary citizen" (Gould 1985: 50). As noted, the Thatcher administration defended such an approach to guard its autonomy from self-serving interest groups, meaning, for the most part, unions. Other self-serving groups continued to enjoy access to and participation in the government's decision-making process.

Such selective rule-making might be justified by some version of social contract theory, provided it has the informed consent of the people affected. But social contract theorists are divided over the status of groups in a just polity. Intended primarily as ways to legitimate a political system, the various contract theories that have been developed are of little use to defenders of a role for private groups in the political public arena. But if a theory espouses political equality then it should endorse a role for politically active groups, because these groups can help achieve it. Such open-ended inclusiveness would be vulnerable, however, to certain objections based on the process of group formation.

First, there is a slippery slope concern that political accommodation of any nongovernment interest group endangers social unity in that it invites countless other groups to claim comparable consideration. But interest groups, as understood in political theory, are by definition operative political entities. So any attempt to deny some group access and voice would without more constitute an arbitrary veto over what social entities can be active in the public arena. Such gate-keeping is standard practice, of course, in a tyranny. But if participatory democracy is an accepted goal, a polity needs to remain open to *emergent* interest groups in addition to politically established groups already recognized. To do so, of course, it might need to modify the status quo. But equal access is not a static concept reducible to the status quo – at least not if a group not yet heard from now seeks to argue for its members' interests in the political public sphere.

An interest group, then, is any organization that acts politically in behalf of those who are associated with it. The number of interest groups in a society is determined not taxonomically but politically. So whether a marginalized group can gain recognition in the political arena depends on multiple factors over which it may have little control, notably, the tolerance of those that already have access and voice. At best, their acceptance will be determined by collective deliberations that address its claims along with those of others. At worst, they will be systematically excluded from political power (if not deported). Such was the situation in which Catholics found themselves in post-Reformation England, nor did the theoretical populist John Locke see any reason to fault such discrimination (Cranston 1987: 104, 109). Would he also wink at the discrimination experienced in our day by such groups as the indigenous Palestinians in Israel?

As Zionists made Judaism the basis for a nation-state in land long inhabited by the Palestinians, they scarcely acknowledged the latter's existence. Many thousands of the latter were forced to flee the country during the war that followed the establishment of Israel (1947-49). As for those who remained, Israeli political leaders ironically treat them as Jews had been treated in countries from which they emigrated (Evron 1995). This undemocratic dominance is, however, becoming less feasible as new political parties emerge to represent the various heretofore unrepresented interests in Israel. Setting an example for the indigenous Arabs in Israel, later Jewish immigrants from the Soviet Union formed a political party to represent their interests, and some of these latecomers have been elected to the Israeli parliament.

Similar developments have occurred in other countries. A group called the Committee for Fairness has been formed in eastern Germany to defend the interests of people long resident there against discriminatory policies of the post-reunification State. In the United States, a group called Compassion in Dying has been formed to assist in voluntary suicides of the terminally ill, and a National Breast Cancer Coalition seeks increased federal funding for research on that long neglected disease. Meanwhile, long established groups of all kinds look after the interests of their members: Old Etonians in the UK and its Yale University counterpart, Skull and Bones; the Committee to Defend the Workers (KOR) in Poland, and Freemasons in many countries. Such relatively new groups as the American Gourd [Growers] Society and the Central Intelligence [Agency] Retirees Association do the same for their members.

Similarly, many religious interest groups, especially in the United States (Jones and Weber 1994), engage in philanthropic activity that differs little from what a secular group might do, e.g., the Quaker-based American Friends Service Committee.

Other religion-based groups provide an essentially secular service but also steer users to a religious activity, e.g., the Salvation Army. There are also a growing number of religious groups that are politically active and, accordingly, are better known because of media exposure. These include policy-oriented groups, e.g., the Christian Coalition, the National Association of Evangelicals, Focus on the Family, the Family Research Council, and American Values, as well as groups that organize demonstrations in behalf of causes they embrace.

The specific causes that religious groups pursue run the gamut of mainstream political acceptability. Moreover, some religious groups have a more explicitly political agenda than others. On some occasions they might all be active in the political arena, as when they all came out in support of the (irresponsibly unfunded) Leave No Child Behind Act of 2002. Sometimes an activist religion-based group runs into law enforcement and courtroom challenges. This is especially the case with efforts to block a woman's right to have an abortion, which is the focus of such groups as Operation Rescue and Concerned Women for America.

As regards any other group that pursues an agenda, an activist religious group might well be faulted for not imposing limits on the tactics to which its members are advised to use. Blood-shedding and bullying are particularly repugnant, no matter how righteous the perpetrator may feel about his or her cause. Apart from such violations of civility and decency, a religious group is surely entitled to exercise the same rights of speech and assembly that others enjoy. To deny them these rights in principle would arguably give those that already enjoy access and voice inordinate control over the list of social concerns that merit consideration. To assert that their members' perceptions of special need justify no special representation is to make the abstract individual of egalitarian theory a substitute for the diverse participants who rub elbows in the day-to-day process of building democracy.

Meaningful egalitarianism, in other words, must be contextual and dynamic, that is, open to meeting needs too long neglected. This, in turn, is precisely the point at which an emerging interest group might call attention to real needs that society at large has failed to meet. Among these unmet needs are, e.g., those of the unemployed, disabled war veterans, an insolvent company that employs many people and provides a needed product or service, a neglected indigenous tribe, retirees, people with renal failure or a foreclosure on their mortgage. In the interest of what some call vertical equity, such unequally situated people should be treated in appropriately unequal ways, for example, by means of "special legislation."

The foregoing is perhaps the standard model of an interest group, that is, it espouses the interests of its constituents in the political sphere. These interests are typically based on special needs, so their recognition in public policy may apply only to the represented group and perhaps others similarly situated. Though selective, such recognition is likely to be remedial and compensatory, so anyone who perceives it to be for the public good should not consider it unfair. Those whose perception differs may, of course, disagree. To see this, just compare people's attitude towards such varied interest group beneficiaries as children (born and/or unborn), family-owned dairies, savings and loan institutions, Wall Street investment brokers, veterans of foreign wars, sex-trafficked women, black lung sufferers, the developmentally disabled, and illegal immigrants. But as the UN has come to recognize, the quality of policy decisions is inevitably improved if responsible issue-focused advocacy groups participate in the policy making process.

There are, in short, good reasons for endorsing many interest groups' political activism, whatever their underlying beliefs, provided what they seek is not detrimental to the larger community's well-being. Practical considerations favor supporting such groups insofar as they help correct an overly undifferentiated view of social reality and as such do not discredit egalitarian principles. More generally, some interest groups' efforts to influence policy do benefit the general public, e.g., when consumer groups lobby for stronger controls over contaminated food products, or a lawyers' organization seeks to have the excesses of mandatory sentencing modified. Problems arise, however, when a zero-sum game is involved, i.e., when an interest group – be it religious or not – pursues political favors that in advantaging its constituents would thereby directly disadvantage other people without just cause.

The expressions 'directly disadvantage' and 'without just cause' are crucial here. For, in response to interest-group lobbying a government body might approve a narrowly targeted benefit that neither directly disadvantages others nor is unjustifiable because the people at large should approve, e.g., providing adequate health care to wounded veterans, subsidizing otherwise unprofitable orphan drugs. On the other hand, benefits directed to special interests may harm others directly and be otherwise unjustifiable. This arguably happens, e.g., when a bill going through Congress is loaded down with earmarks, i.e., provisions added to a bill without debate to fund projects that benefit only elected officials' contributors.

More broadly, massive special favors involving billions of dollars are to be expected when an organization that represents large corporations, e.g., the National Manufacturers Association, uses its influence to affect public policy. So in this context political decisions all too often simply disregard fairness and respect for the rights of the ordinary citizen. This, however, does not justify analogous influencing on the part of religious groups when they seek to persuade lawmakers to institute policies that they favor even though such policies are arguably, even manifestly, contrary to the well-being of many people who lack comparable political influence. In this regard, I call attention to domestic policy lobbying to criminalize abortion and foreign policy lobbying to start a war.

Debate regarding choice has, of course, been intense in the United States since the U.S. Supreme Court ruled in 1971 that early-stage abortions are constitutionally permissible. This decision (*Roe v. Wade*) brought forth activist opposition that has managed to limit the decision's scope in various ways, e.g., by requiring a minor to obtain parental notification. In the process, so-called pro-life advocates have mounted advertising campaigns that refer to abortionists as "baby killers" and show pictures of fetuses to demonstrate that they are "human beings." Such visual and terminological mis-communication most definitely originates in the offices of organizations that represent conservative Christian believers. But, pace liberal scholars who debate appropriate public arena discourse, it is not per se religious. It is simply misleading and inflammatory. So also are the background arguments that pro-life academics produce as though to demonstrate the manifest rationality of efforts to ban abortions.

One such author, a Catholic philosopher, proceeds as follows. First he claims that secularists, in seeking to make abortion legal, thereby assert that aborting a fetus is moral, and in the process impose "this key belief of secularism on those who disagree with it." If abortion is legalized, its opponents are coerced by a law that they find abhorrent; and so they seek to have abortions of "these youngest members of the human family" banned on grounds comparable to that of abolitionists who sought to have slavery eliminated (Sweetman 2006: 136-137, 175-177,192-193). This analogy is traceable to a legal scholar who views pro-life activism as a continuation of the nineteenth century abolitionist movement (Carter 2000: 69-70, 89, 109-110). In other words, on this view, preventing a fetus (only arguably a human being) from being expelled from a uterus is morally equivalent to freeing a slave (unquestionably a human being). But in taking up this issue, be it noted, one is not called upon to determine whether any religious language (there is none) ought to be excluded. This noted, one might further wish to ponder over the fact that the first author here cited concedes that a case could be made for legalizing euthanasia (Sweetman 2006: 190); and, moreover, that the moral authorities of the author's religion have recently allowed their constituents to vote for a pro-choice candidate for public office (NYT 11/15/07, A30).

Troublesome as one might find the religion-based efforts to criminalize all abortions, that activity pales in comparison to the, unfortunately, more successful effort on the part of pro-Israel individuals and groups to persuade the U.S. government to support Israel's military preferences in the Middle East, including the U.S. invasion and occupation of Iraq. That this lobbying effort did in fact take place with regard to the war against Iraq in particular is neither widely known nor often acknowledged. But there is a substantial body of evidence to that effect (Mearsheimer and Walt 2007:

Part II). This evidence involves influential activists who, whether tied to a synagogue or not, are religiously dedicated to supporting Israel's every regional preference and its every request for money and materiel, including nuclear weapons.

Several lobbying groups stand out as being most actively dedicated to making Israel's needs known to the US government. These include the Zionist Organization of America (ZOA), the American Israel Public Affairs Committee (AIPAC), the Washington Institute for Near East Policy, the Anti-Defamation League, and Christians United for Israel (CUFI). Other groups and individuals have been supportive over the years, but recently some American Jews have openly adopted a less uniformly pro-Israel stance (NYT 4/25/2008). Taken as a whole, however, this network of support is so longstanding and so uncritical that anyone who dares question a particular project is immediately branded an anti-Semite. This tactic has kept elected officials quite thoroughly in check over the sixty years since the founding of the State of Israel (Mearsheimer and Walt 2007: ch. 6).

The extent to which the worldview of these various groups deserves to be identified as religious is a matter of interpretation in some respects. But for different reasons both the ZOA and the CUFI are clearly religion-based. In other respects, all are ethnically selective, i.e., they are unhesitatingly open to ethnic discrimination vis-à-vis Palestinians whether within or already fled from land occupied by Israel. For these and other reasons, a strong case could be made for limiting the ability of the pro-Israel lobby to exercise the kind of influence it now enjoys. There is in fact some organized effort to do just that.

Leaving aside these controversial questions about the propriety of limiting advocacy, I turn now to some final remarks directed to the concerns of philosophers. These have to do with sorting out the merits of proposing a ban on all abortions or a war against Iraq. Contrary to the tenor of much philosophical discussion about religious speech in the public arena, the merits of either of these proposals should be determined not by critiquing its proponents' language usage as such (rhetorical excess aside). Rather should the merits of these proposals be determined by whether what they are lobbying is for the good of society at large or only for that of constituents of theirs who feel, respectively, that abortion should never be permitted or that Israel's preferences should never be curtailed.

A full discussion of the proposal to ban abortions would require consideration of the harm caused by rape, incest, severely abnormal offspring, the impoverishment of single mothers, and the punitive character of much domestic law and its agents. A full discussion of pro-Israel policy would require serious questioning of a predominantly militaristic approach to dealing with competing nation-states in the Middle East with a heavy emphasis on the harms caused by war. Here, though, in concluding, I will only say for the record that such are the concerns one should take into account before assessing whether and how religion may impinge on the state.

What all these reflections come down to saying is, to rephrase a constitutional law principle, is that what people think and believe should be entirely their prerogative; the actions they choose or at least plan to perform may, depending on their risk of harming others, be subject to monitoring and as necessary prevention. Between thoughts and deeds, of course, are words; and the least dangerous words are those uttered openly for any and all to hear. This being the case, the form in which a religious group expresses itself in the public arena should rarely be a matter of concern. It matters greatly, however, how thoroughly the objectives it seeks are examined in all their ramifications before these are transformed into state-mandated restrictions or obligations attaching to people at large be they compatible believers or not. For, however much anyone tries to turn his or her wishes into horses, those horses must not be allowed to run rampant over others who happen to get in their way. Nor is it enough to delude these innocents into believing that they are in fact blessed by the opportunity to be thus run over.

This situation of being run over without comprehending why calls to mind another metaphor, that of dramatic irony. Dramatic irony is at work when select spectators know why events are unfolding as they are even though the participants in those events do not know. This selective deception is at times a clever device on a stage for thespians. It is never inherently advantageous, however, to people who with no advance planning on their part just find themselves on the stage of human history. Human history is nonetheless rich in examples of different attitudes and perspectives that people take to heart, relate to as having religious significance, and draw upon to inspire their efforts to better the world in which they live. Without accepting these influences at face value the societies in which they arise have much to gain by remaining open to the possibility that a worldview however different from most people's customary beliefs can make a significant contribution to the general well-being of all.

Summary and Conclusion

We have traveled some distance in these pages. I hope you the reader have come along for the ride in reasonable comfort and are none the worse for wear. I neither want nor expect you to agree with me in every respect if at all. But I would like to think I've made the issues clear along the way so you can now join the discussion and form your own opinions for the years ahead. So before I turn off my word machine let me tell you what I think we've been talking about and why I think it matters.

My one overarching conclusion is that society at large is better off to the extent that state/religion relations remain conciliatory, cooperative, and communicative. Stating this negatively, little is gained politically or socially and much is lost where the state guards against any and all input from religion-oriented sources and, inversely, where religion-oriented people must be on their guard against any contact with the state. To defend this position I first point out that it is not given much support in academic dialogue but is in fact broadly supported by decisions of courts in the United States, especially the U.S. Supreme Court. Then I move beyond these sources to argue on the basis of group rights theory that religious groups, understood as groups, should enjoy more freedom of activity than either academic or juridical thinking has yet endorsed.

Admittedly, this call for openness between the state and religion may sound utopian and in some respects may be so for the foreseeable future (in some countries, undoubtedly, more than in others). Moreover, history provides ample evidence that attempts at state/religion collaboration were often disastrous in their consequences. This was especially the case where multiple religions or denominations of a religion co-existed in the same or in an adjoining jurisdiction. Thus the incongruity of so-called religious wars. It was precisely to put an end to such seemingly endless turmoil that neutrality as to worldview preference became the standard solution to problems associated with the role of religion in the public sphere.

The process of institutionalizing this state neutrality in one country after another was preceded by theoretical efforts to show why a noncommital and at the same time non-adversarial stance towards religion was desirable. Moreover, the extent to which a state achieved this neutral stance was taken to be a sign of its modernity and, by implication, its maturity. Neutrality as to religious preference, however, turned out not to be a panacea. There was, after all, more to a religion than just a banner to identify warriors' commitments.

Religious people at home and abroad engaged in many activities that benefitted others regardless of their religious beliefs. Proselytism was indeed a problem in some situations, notably where colonial arrangements led the "do-gooders" to presume that their worldview was intrinsically preferable to that of their beneficiaries. But as often as not genuinely charitable motives were at work as people reached out to aid others who, for whatever reason, had need of their services. Such social outreach was eventually incorporated into public sector institutions, but never to the extent that the voluntary efforts of sectarian organizations became superfluous. So why couldn't the state look to the results more than the motivating sentiments and accommodate the religious as well as the secular and/or governmental service provider? Moreover, why couldn't the state take advantage of insights that politically active religionists were in a position to provide? These questions, in multiple ramifications, were at the core of considerations regarding state/religion relations throughout the twentieth century.

As noted in the Introduction, efforts to resolve these questions regarding state/religion relations have taken place on several levels. On one level (academic) words are the principal tool. On another level (political) actions are more important. In between these two levels, there is an intermediate level, that of the courts, whose function in these matters has been to express in words with legal force what actions are permissible as between state and religion. Concentrating on developments in the

United States, I reviewed the output of these diverse yet interconnected sources, drew on each of them, and went further to show the insights one can gain by studying religion with respect to its being embodied in groups.

Academic discourse regarding the proper role of religion vis-à-vis the state has for the most part viewed the state as better off without input from religious sources. To make the case for this exclusionary stance, its proponents endorse secularism as the appropriate worldview for public arena discourse; and, as a corollary, they find the discourse prevalent among religious people to be politically inappropriate. This is the starting point from which mainstream scholars have considered whether any accommodation of religious discourse might be admitted into the public arena. Not surprisingly, they have found little room for leeway. Some scholars have recognized, however, that religious people might well have something relevant to say however atypically they say or justify it. So, these scholars have suggested, religious talk that arguably has political merit may be given a temporary permit while its utterer comes up with some secular translation of his or her message.

This is hardly what one might call an open door policy. But it is here one must start if one wishes to argue that religious people deserve more opportunity to be heard than is presently the case. To this end, I examined court rulings and group rights. But before taking up these larger motifs I examined the secular stance in more detail. First I granted that some limits on religious freedom are altogether appropriate but opposed generalizing this constraint. Then I showed that secularism unchallenged is not necessarily neutral but may take positions in its own right and thereby go to extremes as great as those meant to be prevented by official neutrality.

To illustrate why a purportedly religious group might need to be constrained by government action, I discussed the Jonestown massacre. This tragedy defies easy explanation but it certainly involves a group whose understanding of religion was destructive and ultimately indefensible. So there were good reasons for the government to intervene, though it did so too late. Other subsequent interventions are more difficult to justify. So there is clearly a need for "rules of engagement" in these cases.

As it happens, the U.S. Supreme Court has endorsed various limits on religious groups for the sake of good order in society. In many cases, the limits endorsed have been quite moderate. But cases that dealt with more serious matters, e.g., conscientious objection, are by their very nature more complicated. In such cases court rulings that approve but still seek to circumscribe the state's interference into one's religious life are, however decided, controversial. By way of an addendum, it should be remembered that these state intrusions have not uniformly singled out religious groups but sometimes involve a secular group whose activities are deemed disruptive of public order, e.g., the American Communist Party.

The fact that a secular group might be deemed disruptive of public order takes on added weight if secularism is said to be the official doctrine of government itself. This choice of a secular guide is, in turn, typically explained as a non-controversial way to govern in a pluralist society in which only neutrality constitutes a politically correct position. As I went on to show, however, this neutrality is typically honored in the breach as the allegedly neutral government turns neutrality itself into a kind of religion, called by one writer "constitutional faith." Neutrality, on this view, is associated with secularism, which is itself tied to rationalism, by which is meant a dedicated reliance on human reason unaided by any extraneous influence.

Rationalism thus understood is considered by its proponents to be the sole incontrovertible bastion of truth. So they think it should immunize its spokespersons from criticism however extreme their recommendations might be. A special branch of rationalism is scientism, that is, unreflective reliance on science as the sole reputable approach to solving any problem one might face. Scientism commonly manifests itself as an ingenuous appeal to the need for scientific proof as a way of opposing altogether reasonable proposals that challenge some vested interest, e.g., to stop industrial pollution that is endangering people's health. This subterfuge, I also noted, is routinely used to discredit opponents of any military endeavor however costly in terms of money or lives. Now that our world includes innumerable nuclear weapons and the potential for their spread, such use of scientism to preserve the politico-economic status quo risks becoming the fast track to Armageddon.

Mandatory secularism, as I call it, was favored by a number of governments throughout much of the twentieth century. But this did not prevent secular governments from using religions for their own ends. In any event, such governance is no longer widely favored. American secularists, however, have remained steadfast in their efforts to make secularism the mindset of preference for any self-respecting polity. Similarly, various religions have sought to be recognized as uniquely suited to the modern world because they are in some fashion science-based. With or without such grounds for credibility, the cash value of a religion remains largely in the eye of the beholder. The beholder, though, is on many occasions a court deciding a case to maintain state/religion border control.

In the United States, the lodestone of state/religion border control is the First Amendment, especially via its free exercise (of religion) and its nonestablishment clauses. Favoring the former is called accommodationism. Favoring the latter is called separationism. In practice, the Court long assigned preeminence to separation, but recently it has been shifting towards accommodation. Particularly as regards education, this change in constitutional jurisprudence marks the denouement of a period during which secularism prevailed in public schools and American Catholics chose alternative schooling to facilitate maintenance of their religious values.

Throughout most of the twentieth century the U.S. Supreme Court consistently handed down separationist rulings with regard to K-12 public education. Meanwhile, it opposed accommodating state support of most but not all secular functions of religion-oriented schools. A key exception to separation involved the "child benefit" theory, e.g., to fund schoolbooks. Inversely, some religious uses of public school property have been allowed, e.g., to hold a meeting or show a movie. Such exceptions may become more typical as religion-sponsored schools face financial problems that risk adding thousands of students to the public school rosters.

The gorilla in the room in this regard is the American Catholic parochial school system. It began early in the nineteenth century as an antidote to Protestant influences in the public schools. Then it blossomed as secularism became the prevailing though often tested worldview in public schools. Its financial base consisted of an abundance of minimally paid nuns and some lay teachers, the vast majority of whom have no successors as women find many more employment opportunities in the wider world.

Assuming students' maturity on the college level, the Court seldom felt a need to address state-religion issues on this level. Secularism was commonly the norm among academics. Where it was not, e.g., mandatory chapel, such religion favoring practices gradually died out. Meanwhile, the Catholic hierarchy sought value maintenance via clerical presence on secular campuses and touting Catholic institutions of higher learning. These efforts have been of limited avail as Catholic youth persist in attending whatever college offers the programs that best fit their career aspirations.

As the preceding chapter in alternative education comes to an end, unprecedented stresses to public sector budgets require opening a new chapter. This new chapter may well take the form of more state-religion collaboration to limit costs to state and local governments. To succeed, though, this new chapter will require government to be a partner in support of alternative education, especially as provided by charter schools. These state-supported K-12 schools will have various sponsors that agree only on the inadequacy of a standard public school education. Among these are, for example, secularists, Protestants, and Muslims as well as Catholics. Their programs will challenge the flexibility of the Court, to be sure. But having recently busied itself with rulings that bolster federalism, i.e., empowering non-federal governmental actors, it has already laid the juridical groundwork for needed accommodations.

This speculation on my part about the future of state/religion relations in education is put forth on a strictly "time will tell" basis. The same could no doubt be done with regard to state-religion relations in the politics of the public sphere. In lieu of such a daring venture, I merely developed a philosophical argument for why religion should have a place in such political activity. This argument consists of a three-step application of group rights theory to religious groups. This involves showing that interest groups are politically important, groups as such are morally important, and accordingly that religious groups are both politically and morally important.

To bring out the political importance of groups I drew on the views of various political theorists, e.g., Durkheim, de Tocqueville, Arendt, Dewey, and Galbraith. After noting how political action committees constitute a link between people and politicians, I added the pro-group arguments of legal scholar Owen Fiss and philosopher Will Kymlicka. Taken together, these and other like-minded scholars challenge liberals' reliance on individual initiative in favor of collective action.

To further dissipate liberals' individualist outlook, I next argued that because individuals are responsible for the world around them it is morally necessary for them to participate in one or another group for the sake of the common good. To this end I showed how the absence of such moral collaboration in Kew Gardens contributed to the death of Kitty Genovese. With these reflections in the background, I then considered various difficulties that weaken the case for collective responsibility.

These difficulties involve various anti-egalitarian arrangements, such as an overarching decision-maker not treating all petitioning groups fairly. Other challenges arise if people who are organized are favored over people who are not, or if some groups enjoy higher status or are otherwise more effective than is true of other groups, or if some groups have access to more resources than do others, or if a group however effective mistreats its own members, or if groups become so numerous as to impede their separate or combined effectiveness.

Equipped with these thoughts about politically active groups, I then addressed the thorny question of religious toleration, i.e, how a government goes about accommodating religious groups that seek fair treatment and as need be a fair hearing before that government. For many centuries such openness, if exercised at all, was selective. Only much later was pluralism taken to be a given that requires a more flexible response. In particular, diverse religious groups should have the ability to function as or (to safeguard relevant tax exempt status) to form or contribute to an interest group in order to bring its concerns before a governing jurisdiction.

De facto there are many such religion-based interest groups at work in the United States. The causes for which they seek a favorable political response are varied, some being generally palatable to the public at large, others perhaps less so. Especially troubling to many outsiders are the calls of ultra-conservative religious interest groups for a ban on all abortions or for open-ended support of any cause dear to the Israeli government. One's opposition to such controversial quests should not be based, I maintain, on the fact that the questing group has religious ties. Rather should it be based as with any other interest group on arguments in opposition to the specific public policy that the group espouses.

REFERENCES

Archard, David, ed. (1996) *Philosophy and Pluralism*. Cambridge: Cambridge University Press.

Anton, Anatole, Milton Fisk, and Nancy Holmstrom, eds. (2000) *Not For Sale: In Defense of Public Goods*. Boulder, CO: Westview.

Arendt, Hannah (1963) *On Revolution*. New York: Viking.

-----. (1958) *The Origins of Totalitarianism*, 2nd ed. New York: Meridian; orig. 1951.

Audi, Robert (2000) *Religious Commitment and Secular Reason*. Cambridge/New York: Cambridge University Press.

Bedau, Hugo Adam, ed. (1969) *Civil Disobedience: Theory and Practice*: New York/Indianapolis: Bobbs-Merrill Pegasus.

Bellah, Robert. (1992) *The Broken Covenant*, 2nd ed. Chicago: University of Chicago Press.

Blum, Lawrence (2002) *"I'm Not a Racist, But..." The Moral Quandary of Race*. Ithaca: Cornell University Press.

Breuilly, John (1985) *Nationalism and the State*. Manchester: Manchester University Press.

Bridges, Thomas. (1994) *The Culture of Citizenship: Inventing Postmodern Civic Culture* (Albany: State University of New York Press).

Brown, Colin. (1974) *Philosophy and the Christian Faith*. London: Inter-Varsity Press; orig. 1969.

Brown, Jim (2004) "Harvard Study Finds Charter Schools Outperform Public Schools," Agape Press, Sept. 17, posted at http://news.christiansunite.com/religion/religionprint.cgi?1545.

Burleigh, Michael (2007). *Sacred Causes: The Clash of Religion and Politics, from the Great War to the War on Terror*. New York: Harper Collins.

Butler, Judith (1990) *Gender Trouble: Feminism and the Subversion of Identity*. London: Routledge.

Byrne, Edmund (1990) *Work, Inc.: A Philosophical Study*. Philadelphia: Temple University Press.

Carter, Stephen L. (2000) *God's Name in Vain*. New York: Basic Books.

-----. (1993) *The Culture of Disbelief*. New York: Basic Books.

Casanova, José. (1994) *Public Religions in the Modern World*. Chicago: University of Chicago Press.

Cawson, Alan (1985) *Organized Interests and the State*. London: Sage.

Chidester, David (2003) *Salvation and Suicide: Jim Jones, The Peoples Temple, and Jonestown*, rev. ed. Bloomington and Indianapolis: Indiana University Press; orig. 1988.

Cohen, Carl. (1971) *Civil Disobedience*. New York: Columbia University Press.

Cohn, Carol. (1987) "Sex and Death in the Rational World of Defense Intellectuals," *Signs* 12:4 (Summer) 687-718.

Cranston, Maurice. (1987) "John Locke and the Case for Tolerance," in Mendus and Edwards 1987: 101-21.

DesAutels, Peggy, Margaret P. Battin, and Larry May (1999) *Praying for a Cure: When Medical and Religious Practices Conflict*. Boulder: Rowman & Littlefield.

Domke, David, and Kevin Coe (2008) *The God Strategy: How Religion Became a Political Weapon in America*. Oxford: Oxford University Press.

Donahue, William A.(1994) *Twilight of Liberty: The Legacy of the ACLU*. London: Transaction.

----- (1985) *The Politics of the American Civil Liberties Union*. New Brunswick: Transaction.

Durkheim, Emile (1997) *The Division of Labor in Society*. New York: Free Press; orig. 1893.

----- (1959) *Socialism and Saint-Simon*, tr. C. Sattler. Yellow Springs, OH: Antioch.

Ellis, John Tracy (1955) "Catholic Intellectual Life in America Today" *Thought*, Fall.

Evron, Boas. (1995) *Jewish State or Israeli Nation?* Bloomington and Indianapolis: Indiana University Press; orig. 1988.

Farrell, John. J. (1907) "The Catholic Chaplain at the Secular University," *CEAB* 4 (Nov. 1907): 150-63.

Feinberg, Joel (1991) "The Moral and Legal Responsibility of the Bad Samaritan," in *The Spectrum of Responsibility*, ed. Peter A. French (New York: St. Martin's Press):148-69.

----- (1990) "Autonomy and Community," ch. 29A of *Harmless Wrongdoing (The Moral Limits of the Law*, vol. 4), pp. 81-123. New York: Oxford University Press; orig. 1987.

Figgis, John Neville (1997) *Churches in the Modern State, 2nd ed.* Bristol, UK: Thoemmes Press; orig. 1914.

Fishkin, James (1982) *The Limits of Obligation*. New Haven: Yale University Press.

Fitt, Lord. (1987) "Toleration in Northern Ireland," in Mendus and Edwards 198: 63-82.

Fussell, Paul. (1989) "The Real War 1939-1945," *Atlantic Monthly* (Aug.) 32-48.

Galbraith, John Kenneth (1963) *American Capitalism*, rev. ed. (Middlesex: Penguin).

Galston, William (1991) *Liberal Purposes: Goods, Virtues, and Diversity in the Liberal State*. Cambridge: Cambridge University Press.

Gould, Brian (1985) *Socialism and Freedom*. London: Macmillan.

Greenawalt, Kent. (1995) *Private Consciences and Public Reasons*. New York: Oxford University Press.

Habermas, Jürgen (1989) *The Structural Transformation of the Public Sphere*, tr. Thomas Burger et al. Cambridge, MA: MIT Press; orig. 1962.

----- (1983) *Philosophical-Political Profiles*, tr. Frederick G. Lawrence. London: Heinemann; orig. 1971.

Hamilton, Marci A. (2007) *God vs. the Gavel: Religion and the Rule of Law*. Cambridge, UK: Cambridge University Press; orig. 2005.

Hill, Paul T., ed (2006) *Charter Schools against the Odds: An Assessment of the Koret Task Force on K-12 Education*. Stanford: Hoover Press.

Hixson, Richard F. (1987) *Privacy in a Public Society: Human Rights in Conflict.* New York: Oxford University Press.

Hofrenning, Daniel J. B. (1995) *In Washington But Not of It: The Prophetic Politics of Religious Lobbyists* (Philadelphia: Temple University Press).

Hook, Sidney (1970) *The Paradoxes of Freedom.* Berkeley: University of California Press.

Ingram, David (2000) *Group Rights: Reconciling Equality and Difference.* Lawrence, KS: University Press of Kansas.

Jones, Landis, and Paul J. Weber (1994) *US Religious Interest Groups: Institutional Profiles.* Westport, CT: Greenwood Press.

Juergensmeyer, Mark (1993) *The New Cold War? Religious Nationalism Confronts the Secular World.* Berkeley: University of California Press.

Kymlicka, Will (1989) *Liberalism, Community, and Culture.* Oxford: Oxford University Press.

Kleinberg, Stanley S. (1991) *Politics and Philosophy: The Necessity of Limitations of Rational Argument.* Oxford/Cambridge, MA: Blackwell.

Langston, Mike (2003) "Addressing the Need for a Uniform Definition of Gang-Involved Crime - Perspective," *FBI Law Enforcement Bulletin* (Feb.)

Larmore, Charles (1996) *The Morals of Modernity.* Cambridge: Cambridge University Press.

Lazare, Daniel. (1996) *The Frozen Republic.* New York: Harcourt Brace.

Lecky, William E. H. (1955) *History of European Morals: From Augustus to Charlemagne.* New York: Braziller; orig. 1869.

Levinson, Sanford. (1988) *Constitutional Faith.* Princeton: Princeton University Press.

Levy, Leonard W. (1994) *The Establishment Clause*, 2nd ed. rev. Chapel Hill, NC: University of North Carolina Press; orig. 1986.

----- (1993) *Blasphemy.* New York: Knopf.

Loucks, Orie L.. (1972) "Systems Methods in Environmental Court Actions," ch. 10 in *Systems Analysis and Simulation in Ecology*, ed. Bernard C. Patten (New York: Academic Press), 419-73.

-----. (1971) "The Trial of DDT in Wisconsin," in *Patient Earth*, ed. J. Harte and R. H. Socolow (New York: Holt, Rinehart & Winston), ch. 7, pp. 88-107.

MacFarquhar, Neil (2003) "Syria, Long Ruthlessly Secular, Sees Fervent Islamic Resurgence," NYT 24 Oct.

MacIntyre, Alasdair. (1971) *Against the Self-Images of the Age: Essays on Ideology and Philosophy*. London: Duckworth.

Marshall, William P. (1993) "The Other Side of Religion," *Hastings Law Journal* 44: 843.

May, Larry (1987) *The Morality of Groups: Collective Responsibility, Group-Based Harm and Corporate Rights*. Notre Dame: Notre Dame University Press.

Mendus, Susan, and David Edwards, ed. (1987) *On Toleration*. Oxford: Clarendon Press.

Morris, Charles R. (1997) *American Catholic*. New York: Random House Times Book.

Moore, Rebecca. (2005) "Reconstructing Reality: Conspiracy Theories about Jonestown," in *Controversial New Religions*, ed. James R. Lewis and Jesper Aagaard Petersen (Oxford: Oxford University Press, 2005), pp. 61-78.

Mujahid, Abdul Malik (2001) "Muslims in America: Profile 2001." Online at http://www.soundvision.com/info/yearinreview/2001/profile.asp

Murray, John Courtney (1960) *We Hold These Truths: Catholic Reflections on the American Proposition*. New York: Sheed & Ward.

Nagel, Thomas. (1987) "Moral Conflict and Political Legitimacy," *Philosophy and Public Affairs* 16: 215-240.

Numan, Fareed H. (1992) "A Brief Statement," *Islam 101*, online at http://www.islam101.com/history/population2_usa.html

Nussbaum, Martha (1999) "Professor of Parody: The Hip, Defeatist Feminism of Judith Butler," *New Republic* (22 Feb.) 37-45.

NYT: *New York Times*.

Olson, Mancur (1982) *The Rise and Decline of Nations: Economic Growth, Stagflation, and Social Rigidities*. New Haven: Yale University Press.

----- (1971) *The Logic of Collective Action: Public Goods and the Theory of Groups*. Cambridge, MA: Harvard University Press.

OMB Watch (2003) "The USA Patriot Act and its Impact on Nonprofit Organizations," posted online at http://www.ombwatch.org/article/articlereview/1803/1/{category_id}

Osberg, Eric (2006) "Charter School Funding," in Hill (2006), ch. 2, pp. 45-69.

Pakaluk, Michael (1994) "The Liberalism of John Rawls: A Brief Exposition," in *Liberalism at the Crossroads*, ed. C. Wolfe and J. Hittinger. Lanham, MD: Rowman & Littlefield.

Phelan, Shane (1989) *Identity Politics: Lesbian Feminism and the Limits of Community*. Philadelphia: Temple University Press.

Philips, Kevin (2006) *American Theocracy: The Peril and Politics of Radical Religion, Oil, and Borrowed Money in the 21st Century*. New York: Viking.

Pipes, Daniel (2001) "How Many Muslims?" NYT, 29 Oct.

Rawls, John. (1993) *Political Liberalism*. New York: Columbia University Press.

----- (1969) "The Justification of Civil Disobedience," in Bedau 1969: 240-55.

Reardon, Betty (1985) *Sexism and the War System*. New York: Columbia University Teachers College Press.

Reidy, David A. (1999) "Rawls's Idea(l) of Public Reason," *Polis*, Jan.: 93-113.

-----. (2000) "Rawls's Wide View of Religion: Not Wide Enough," *Res Publica* 6: 49-72.

Rémond, René (1999) *Religion and Society in Modern Europe*, tr. Antonia Nevill. Oxford: Blackwell.

Rorty, Richard. (1979) *Philosophy and the Mirror of Nature*. Princeton: Princeton University Press.

Rosen, Jeffrey (2000) "Is Nothing Secular?" NYT Magazine, 30 Jan.

Rosenthal, A. M. (1999) *Thirty-Eight Witnesses: The Kitty Genovese Case*. Berkeley: University of California Press.

Rousseau, Jean Jacques (1954) *The Social Contract*, tr. Willmoore Kendall. Chicago: Regnery Gateway; orig. 1762.

Scarman, Lord. (1987) "Toleration and the Law," in Mendus and Edwards 1987: 49-62.

Shelton, Baxter J. (2004) "A constitutional right to operate sectarian public charter schools? Considerations of free speech and free exercise of religion in California charter schools," Doctoral dissertation, New York: Columbia University.

Sombart, Werner (1937) *A New Social Philosophy*. Princeton: Princeton University Press.

Stapleton, Julia (1995) *Group Rights: Perspectives Since 1900*. Bristol, UK: Thoemmes Press.

Stone, Christopher (1974) *Should Trees Have Standing?* Los Altos, CA: Kaufman.

Sweetman, Brendan (2006) *Why Politics Needs Religion: The Place of Religious Arguments in the Public Square*. Downers Grove, IL: Intervarsity Press IVP Academic.

Tabor, James D., and Eugene V. Gallagher. (1995) *Why Waco? The Battle for Religious Freedom in America* (Berkeley: University of California Press).

Tamir, Yael (1993) *Liberal Nationalism*. Princeton: Princeton University Press.

Thurley, Peter (nd) "A Failed Argument for Moral Realism: Thomas Nagel and Moral Realism as Justification for Liberalism," online at http://~pthurley/index/Nagel.html.

Tocqueville, Alexis de (1988) *The Ancien Régime*, tr. John Bonner. London: J. M. Dent & Sons; Everyman Classic.

Walzer, Michael (1983) *Spheres of Justice: A Defense of Pluralism and Equality*. New York: Basic Books.

Wise, David. (n.d.) "Jonestown, the CIA and the Mystery Tape," online at http://jonestown.sdsu.edu/AboutJonestown/JonestownReport/v7/wise875.htm

Wolff, Robert Paul (1968) *The Poverty of Liberalism*. Boston: Beacon Press.

Young, Iris Marion (1990) *Justice and the Politics of Difference*. Princeton: Princeton University Press.

----- (1986) "Polity and Group Difference: A Critique of the Ideal of Universal Citizenship," *Ethics* 99(2) 250-274.

Young, Shaun P. (2002) "Illusions of Difference? Larmore's Political Liberalism," *Minerva-An Internet Journal of Philosophy* 6:68-102.

Zysman, John (1983) *Government, Markets, and Growth*. Ithaca: Cornell University Press.

Index (* = cited only)

Alabama, 37
America Magazine, 72
American Civil Liberties Union, 29-30
American Communist Party, 100, 120
American Israel Public Affairs Committee (AIPAC), 114
American Family Foundation, 53
American Federation of Teachers, 75
American Friends Service Committee, 109
American Nazi Party, 36-37
American Sign Language, 103
American Socialist Party, 36-37
American Values, 110
Americanism, 68
Amin, Idi, 28
Amish, 33
Anti-Defamation League, 114
Anton, Anatole, et al., 88
Arendt, Hannah, 85
Association of Classical and Christian Schools, 65
Association of Christian Schools International, 65
Audi, Robert, 14-15
Augsburg Interim of 1555, 106
Aung San Suu Kyi, 39

Barber, Benjamin, 88*
Bellah, Robert, 40
Bermuda, 66
Bipartisan Campaign Reform Act of 1971, 87
Blum, Lawrence, 89*
Boston, 68
Boy Scouts of America, 99
Branch Davidians, 29, 53

Breuilly, John, 83*, 84*, 100*
Brewer, Justice David, 53-54
Bridges, Thomas, 21
Brown, Jim, 75*
Buchanan and Tullock, 96*
Burleigh, Michael, 46*
Burma (see Myanmar)
Bush, George W., administration, 99
Butler, Judith, 89
Byrne, Edmund, 87*

Canada, 66, 90, 91
Carter, Stephen L., 14*, 113*
Casanova, José, 18
Catholic University of America, The, 67, 68, 70
Catholicism, 12, 34, 73
Cawson, Alan, 82
Charlemagne, 11
Charter schools, 63, 74-76, 122
Chicago, 69
Chidester, David, 26, 27, 28
Cheney, Vice-President Dick, 99
China, 13, 16, 17, 46
Chomsky, Noam, 46
Christian Coalition, 109
Christian Schools International, 65
Christian Science, 45
Christians United for Israel, 114
Cohen, Carl, 47
Cohn, Carol, 44*
Committee for Fairness, 109
Communism, 28, 35, 45
Compassion in Dying, 109
Concerned Women for America, 110
Conscientious objection (to war), 35-36, 37, 55-56

Constantine, Emperor, 11, 106
Constitution (US), 3, 5, 16, 32, 40, 49, 51, 53, 54, 63, 89, 97
Council of Mind Abuse, 53
Cranston, Maurice, 108*
Cuba, 2
Cult Awareness Network, 53

Declaration of Independence, 37
Declaration of the Rights of Man, 4
Democratic Party, 46
DesAutels, Peggy, et al., 45*
Dewey, John, 86, 123
Domke, David, and Kevin Coe, 16*, 49*
Donahue, William A., 30*
Durkheim, Emile, 81-82, 86, 123

Edict of Milan, 106
Egypt, 17
Eichmann, Adolf, 30
Ellis, John Tracy, Msgr., 72
Engels, Friedrich, 86
Eritrea, 46
Europe, 1, 2, 3, 4, 11, 12, 34, 46, 49
European Union, 3, 16, 103
Evron, Boas, 109

Family Research Council, 110
Farrell, John J., 70*
Federal Election Campaign Act of 1971, 87
Feinberg, Joel, 93, 94
Figgis, John Neville, 105
First Amendment, 4, 18, 29, 30, 31, 32, 35, 36, 43, 49, 51, 53, 55, 70, 77, 79, 187, 89, 121
Fishkin, James, 94*
Fiss, Owen, 89, 123
Fitt, Lord, 107*

Focus on the Family, 110
Freedom of Information Act of 1966, 97
French, Peter, 94*
French Revolution, 17
Freud, Sigmund, 42
Fussell, Paul, 44

Galilei, Galileo, 42, 47
Galbraith, John Kenneth, 86
Galston, William, 17*
Genovese, Kitty, 93-94, 123
Gibbons, Cardinal, 69
Gould, Brian, 107
Gramsci, Antonio, 27
Greenawalt, Kent, 18*, 19
Gutman, Jeremiah S., 29
Guyana, 26-28

Habermas, Jürgen, 85, 100
Hare Krishna, 30
Harr, Jonathan, 43
Harvard University, 69
Hatch Act of 1939, 100
Hedges, Chris, 44
Held, Virginia, 93*
Hill, Paul T., 75*
Hitler, Adolf, 33
Hixson, 97*
Hofrenning, Daniel J. B., 19*, 33*
Hook, Sidney, 46-47

India, 2
Indiana General Assembly, 17
Indonesia, 3
Ingram, David, 93*, 103*
Iowa State University, 71
Iran, 105
Iraq, 21, 107, 113, 114
Ireland, 3

Ireland, Bishop John, 68
Israel, 2, 3, 46, 84, 90, 108-109, 114

Jackson, Justice Robert H., 53
Jehovah's Witnesses, 52
Jones, Landis, and Paul J. Weber, 109
Jones, Rev. Jim, 26-29
Jonestown, 26-29, 119
Juergensmeyer, Mark, 18

Keating Five, 99
Kew Gardens, 123
Kenya National Youth Alliance, 26
Kikuyu, 26
King, Rev. Martin Luther, Jr., 20
Kleinberg, Stanley S., 16*
Koresh, David, 29
Kuhn, Thomas S., 42
Kymlicka, Will, 89, 90-91

Langston, Mike, 26
Laplace, René, 47
Larmore, Charles, 15
Lazare, Daniel, 40
Leave No Child Behind Act of 2002, 110
Lecky, William E. H., 106*
Leo XIII, Pope, 68-69
Levinson, Sanford, 40
Levy, Leonard W., 12*, 106*
Lincoln, Abraham, 20
Little Hatch Acts, 100
Locke, John, 108
Loucks, Orie L., 43*

MacFarquhar, Neil, 13*
Marshall, William P., 13*
Marx, Karl, 27, 28, 45, 85-86
MacIntyre, Alasdaire, 17
Masai, 26

May, Larry, 93*, 94, 102*
Mearsheimer and Walt, 114*
Michigan, University of, 47
Mill, John Stuart, 95
Moon, Rev. Sun Myung, 30
Moore, Rebecca, 27*
Mormonism, 35
Mormons, 31, 52
Morris, Charles R., 68*, 69*, 74*
Mujahid, 76*
Mungiki, 26
Murray, S.J., John Courtney, 72, 73
Muslims, 34, 57, 63, 76, 90, 105, 122
Myanmar/Burma, 3, 17, 46

NAACP, 37
Nagel, Thomas, 15, 16
National Association of Evangelicals, 110
National Breast Cancer Coalition, 109
National Catholic Education Association, 69
National Catholic Welfare Conference, 71
National Manufacturers Association, 112
National Rifle Association, 88
Nazis, 83
Netherlands, The, 105
New Hampshire, 75
Newman, John Henry Cardinal, 69
Newman Clubs, 69, 71, 72
New York, 54, 60, 61, 93
New York City, 43, 54, 60
Niebuhr, Reinhold, 46
North Carolina, 74
Northern Ireland, 107
Numan, 76*
Nussbaum, Martha, 89*

O'Connor, Justice Sandra Day, 31
Olson, Mancur, 101
OMB Watch, 76
Operation Rescue, 110
Osberg, Eric, 75*

Pakaluk, Michael, 19*
Pakistan, 46
Palestinians, 90, 108, 109, 114
Pax Romana, 72
Pennsylvania, 60, 61, 68
Pennsylvania, University of, 69, 72
Pennsylvania Amish, 30
Peoria, Illinois, 65, 68
Phelan, Shane, 90*
Philips, Kevin, 16*, 18*, 33*
Pipes, Daniel, 76
Pius IX, Pope, 66
Pius X, Pope, 69
Pius XI, Pope, 71
Pius XII, Pope, 72
Plenary Councils of Baltimore, 66-67
Pot, Pol, 33
Poughkeepsie Plan, 68
Privacy Act of 1974, 97
Protestant Reformation, 12, 106
Protestantism, 27, 34, 57, 58, 65
Provincial Councils of Baltimore, 66

Rawls, John, 13, 18, 19-22, 41, 46
Reardon, Betty, 45*
Reformation, 12, 106
Reidy, David, 14, 40
Reign of Terror, 13
Religious freedom, 3, 9, 25, 29, 34, 46, 52, 70, 119
Religious Freedom Restoration Act of 1993, 52
Religious Studies, 62
Rémond, 2*, 4*, 12*, 16*, 49*, 105*

Rhode Island, 60
Rights of Man, Declaration of, 4
Roman Catholicism, 12
Rorty, Richard, 47
Rosen, Jeffrey, 49*
Rosenthal, A. M., 93*
Rousseau, Jean-Jacques, 12*
Ruby Ridge, Idaho, 29
Russia, 27, 46
Ryan, Congressman Leo, 28, 29

Salvation Army, 109
San Francisco, 27
Saudi Arabia, 2, 105
Scarman, Lord, 106
Semmelweis, Ignace, 43
Schwarz-Bart, Eric, 27
Scientology, Church of, 31 45
Seventh Day Adventists, 65
Shanker, Albert, 75
Shelton, Baxter J., 76*
Skokie, Illinois, 37
Sombart, Werner, 83*
South Africa, 102
Soviet Union, 2, 13, 16, 45, 80, 84, 103, 109
Spalding, Bishop John Lancaster, 68, 69
Stalin, Josef, 33
Stapleton, Julia, 95*, 105*
Stone, Christopher, 100*
Supreme Court, US, 18, 30, 34, 35-37, 49, 52, 54, 55, 58-59, 62, 75-77, 79, 87, 89, 99, 100, 112, 117, 119, 121
Sweetman, Brendan, 113
Switzerland, 8
Synanon, 31
Syria, 17, 46

Tabor, James D., and Eugene V. Gallagher, 53*
Tamir, 84, 90
Ten Commandments, 59
Thurley, Peter, 15
Tocqueville, Alexis de, 84, 123
Turkey, 2, 3, 17, 57

Unification Church, 30, 52
United States, 3, 4, 16, 18, 19, 21, 26, 30, 32, 34, 39, 40, 49, 51, 53, 56, 58, 63, 65, 67, 68, 69, 70, 76, 79, 86, 87, 91, 105, 109, 112, 117, 118, 121, 123
Vatican City, 12
Vietnam, War in, 55

Waco, Texas, 29
Washington, DC, 17
Washington Institute for Near East Policy, 114
Wasserstrom, Richard, 46
Walzer, Michael, 91
Weber, Max, 45-46
Wicca, Church of, 53
Woburn, Massachusetts, 43
Wolff, Robert Paul, 82

Young, Iris Marion, 16*, 102-103
Zimbabwe, 102
Zionist Organization of America, 113-114
Zionists, 109
Zysman, John, 84*

Edmund F. Byrne

Dr. Edmund F. Byrne, a retired philosophy professor, edits articles in business ethics and writes in that field and in social and political philosophy, focusing on just war theory. After earning an M.A. in philosophy, Dr. Byrne studied for and spent a few years as a parish priest. As a Fulbright grantee, he obtained his doctorate in philosophy at the University of Louvain in Belgium. He taught at Indiana University-Purdue University for 29 years.